Neurodiversity Within A Divided Nation:

The Nerve to Unite

Joseph Martin Stevenson
Jay Finkelman
Bryant Horowitz
Melissa Druckrey
Karen Wilson-Stevenson

Neurodiversity Within A Divided Nation:

The Nerve to Unite

Joseph Martin Stevenson
Jay Finkelman
Bryant Horowitz
Melissa Druckrey
Karen Wilson-Stevenson

Academica Press
Washington – London

Library of Congress Cataloging-in-Publication Data

Names: Stevenson, Joseph Martin; Finkelman, Jay; Horowitz, Bryant; Druckery, Melissa; Wilson-Stevenson, Karen; authors.
Title: *Neurodiversity within a divided nation : the nerve to unite* / Joseph Martin Stevenson, Jay Finkelman, Bryant Horowitz, Melissa Druckrey, Karen Wilson-Stevenson.
Description: Washington : Academica Press, 2019.
Identifiers: Library of Congress Control Number: 2019939713 | ISBN 9781680534870 (hardcover : alk. paper) | ISBN 9781680531633 (pbk : alk. paper)
LC record available at https://lccn.loc.gov/2019939713

"The beginning is the most important work" – **Plato**

"The divine gift from our own mind" - Dr. Ford in Westworld

"Our human diversity challenges can be addressed, galvanized, and resolved by the unraveling, emancipating, and leveraging God's divine gift above our strong supporting shoulders, between our too often ineffectual listening ears, and behind our too frequently short-sighted eyes…we desperately need neurological frameworks and bold new taxonomies for our future as thoughtful and 'thinking-thoroughly-through-throughout' human beings" – JMS, Dallas, TX; February 2016

For each of the five senses (vision, hearing, smell, touch, and taste), discrete natural pathways normally carry sensory information, a signal, to specific regions in the brain (p. 105) Shiraev and Levy in Cross-Cultural Psychology: Critical thinking and Contemporary Applications, 2017.

"The problems of modern life cry out for creative solutions"

– Mel Rhodes

Contents

Dedication: vii

Foreword viii

I Preface, Purpose, and Organization of Our Book 1

II. Our History, Our Crisis, Our Brains, and Our World Challenges 11

III. Cognitive and Cerebral Levitation for Crucial Thought Leadership 33

IV. Higher Learning, Past Psychology Amid Perplexing Phenomenon. 53

V. Brain Matter, Leadership Lobes, and Other Mindful Matters 65

VI. Crucial Thought Leadership, Learning and Logic 75

VII. Neuroscience, Neuro-Diversity and Neuro Disorders 89

VIII. Questions, Challenges and Culmination 93

About the authors: 101

References 103

Appendix - A 113

Appendix - B 159

Dedication:

Dr. Joseph White,
Professor of Psychology and Psychiatry,
University of California at Irvine

Foreword

We begin by suggesting that fruitful living on our beloved Earth is extremely hard work and loving each other requires the unlocking and the emancipation of the human brain – the core cerebral source for advancing human coherence, connectivity, cohesion and civility. The stakes are simply too high for all stakeholders across our country to not respond to the ongoing and escalating crisis of human division and the desperate need for engagement, enlightenment, and acceptance of our human diversity. Although some would agree with Wesley Morris in The New York Times Magazine (2016) that "It's in America's DNA to be Divisive", others would agree with Joel Achenbach and Scott Clement in The Washington Post that "America Really is More Divided Than Ever" (2016). We especially challenge undergraduate students in America who are studying psychology to consider our commentary and narrative in this, hopefully, breakthrough book. While not all the contributors of this book are psychologists, we strongly encourage academic and practitioner psychologists as well as other social scientists to join in our timely framed narrative. Indeed, we offer this as a serious challenge to our modern, anticipatory, and future civilization given the profound, unprecedented and demographic "explosion" described by William Frey in his work, Diversity Explosion.

Despite the numerous laws, policies, rules, practices, statutes, ordinances, mandates and movements that have contributed to the progress and advancement of human diversity over past decades, NBC's Tom Brokaw recently recognized that America has not been as divided since the 1960s. Recent societal revelations suggest the need for a deeper examination of counter-instances. Conditions seen most recently at Google in Silicon Valley on the West Coast relative to human diversity, and on the East Coast in Virginia regarding human division, reflect this need. Since the founding origins of the United States of America, there have been many other events, occurrences, movements, acts, milestones and other attempts to understand and accept the phenomenon of human diversity within the "American psyche". The newest are immigrant borders, travel bans and refugee barriers.

It is now time to understand the dynamics of human diversity, as well as the drivers of human division, from the momentum, impetus, and genesis where the phenomenon should have been anchored from origin: the brain and the human mind – the three-pound gorilla in the room. Do we need new valiant, audacious, and intrepid theories constructed amid this apparent point that is increasingly becoming a public health reality? Neuroscientist David Eagleman (2015) suggests that perception of reality has less to do with what is out there, and more to do with what is in here [the brain].

Our book aims to start dialogue, discourse and discovery about what may be obvious to many but avoided by most – because its forces us to look inward instead of looking outward. We can make such inward observations, through the lens of psychology, cognition, mindfulness, and underleveraged brain capacity amid modern cultural neuroscience. This is critically important – particularly now in this post-national election time marked by widespread amplification of ambiguity, angst, ambivalence, and anger. However, navigating the human mind is hard work, high maintenance, labor-intensive -- and looking outward and is typically easier, and less painful than looking inward.

To more deeply contextualize the content and broadly advocate a sense of mindful urgency of our book, we use the term "crucial thinking" versus "critical thinking" throughout our narrative. We propose fundamental questions and probing questions -- about what we are calling a form of cognitive "levitation" and taxonomical "climbing" (CBDT) -- to think about for purposes of intellectual discourse, not to necessarily seek empirical evidence for now – until appropriate probing research questions are theoretically framed with conceptual frameworks to position mindful inquiry for empirically-based research on substantiated evidence. Thus, the book is about emancipating taxonomical thought leadership from within. We are asking the academy to provide voices in our book to ignite transdisciplinary interests and expertise across the arts, sciences, and the professions.

Our focus on human experiences from everyday relationships with brain diversity has real life relevance to humans and organizations. We offer two examples from the individual and institutional levels-both with revelations. Sapien Labs (2018) recently recognized that "the human brain is an experience dependent organ, its dynamics are as varied as our life experiences. The lab suggests we seek to enhance human well-being through a deep and inclusive understanding of the diversity of the human brain and its function" (https://sapienlabs.co). Khalil Smith and David Rock (2018) with the Wharton School at the University of Pennsylvania, in "Approaching Diversity with the Brain in Mind", suggest that "for many diversity efforts, raising awareness is assumed to be the natural solution. Afterall, making diversity a priority feels tangible. Pulled in by the immediacy, organizations focus on the prioritization rather than the hard work of behavior change – an approach that's amorphous, complicated to implement, and difficult to measure" (strategy-business.com). Katherine Reynolds Lewis (2014) earlier supported these two revelations in her essay The Next Frontier in Workplace Diversity: Brain Differences, that "a burgeoning civil rights movement is poised to change the workplace and revolves around brain function" (fortune.com).

A special feature of this book is the inclusion of sample student learning outcomes as "provisos" throughout the narrative. When and where student learning outcomes are considered, several elements should be followed. First, student learning outcomes should be composed with lucid clarity and alignment with the curriculum. Second, any ability, skill, disposition, competence or knowledge base driven by the outcome should be measurable in terms of what can be validated, verified or vetted. Thus, student learning outcomes should home in on what students can demonstrate, do, exemplify or exhibit. Third, student learning outcomes, especially related to diversity, should be academically rigorous, personally relevant and socially responsive to a challenging situation or condition relating to human diversity. We have attempted to integrate the student learning outcomes in the text's narrative and connect them to the sections where they are inserted for the reader. The embedded taxonomies in the book can also facilitate the instruction, composition, and conceptualization of targeted student learning outcomes.

The authors of this book include a former provost, a psychologist, a librarian, a brain scientist, and an educator in higher education. Our scholium of brain diversity predates the recent national elections and was presented to the White House Initiatives on Historically Black Colleges and Universities (HBCUs) in 2015 by one of the authors. It is hoped that our "neuro novo" (novo from Latin for new, compound de novo meaning anew) metaphorical book will also begin transdisciplinary dialogue, discourse and discussion about new psychology, cognition, mindfulness, neuroscience, neurodiversity, and brain theory about the power and empowerment of diversity. We call for the power and empowerment of disruption. We want to build on past knowledge bases, revelations in the present literature, contemporary constructs in the global academy, voids or gaps in the academic research, and emerging global conversations.

J.M. Stevenson, Spring, 2017

I
Preface, Purpose, and Organization of Our Book

Caveat #1: ***"First comes thought; then organization of that thought, into ideas and plans; then transformation of those plans into reality. The beginning, as you will observe, is in your imagination."***

- Napoleon Hill

Given the demonstrated leadership of younger people these days, we especially challenge undergraduate students in America who are studying psychology, the social sciences, human resources, the humanities, and theology to consider our commentary and narrative in this, hopefully, breakthrough book. This book draws from a myriad of references, information resources, media source outlets, and other academic publications that, hopefully, will build the case for much needed additional research in brain diversity by other scholars in the field. It is also hoped that this book will be the genesis for starting a conversation about voids in the research, gaps from theory into practice, and unaddressed questions about the mysteries between the brain and human behavior amidst our troubling times of growing social and human divide. There is, indeed, so much to learned about how the brain works, how the brain navigates behavior, and how behavior intersects with the emergent complexities of human diversities. We hope this book will start new conversations, new dialogues, and new thought leadership, especially now in America where there appears to be increasing diversion, disparity and disengagement between and among people.

We have chosen our book sub-title, "The Nerve to Unite" for two primary reasons. One reason is more physiological in explanation, while the other rationale is more philosophical in nature. The nervous system in all humans transmits certain sensations and impulses from the brain and the brain's functionality is central to our book's ultimate intent, message and advocacy. Interestingly, when many humans make references to having "the nerve" to do something, it is often contextualized with a person's convictions or courage from taking a stance on something. We believe this dual definition of "the nerve" conceptualizes the content and context of our book. Although our book is not written in the traditional academic scope, we believe our book content and context provide both traditionally academic and non-traditionally academic audiences to consider the genesis for generating their own convictions, courage and stance from the impulse, sensations and neurons of their brains. This gives the book and its readers, especially undergraduates, the opportunities and openings for contributing to national conversations about our emerging division and about our growing human divisiveness amid intensifying cultural diversity throughout our country. Our hope is the genesis generated among all of us can help to find positive answers, responses and reactions to our present human divides, divisions, disparities, and disengagements. Can the mindful impulses, sensations and messages to the human brain that drive racist, sexist, or homophobic attitudes, dispositions, and behaviors be leveraged to the opposite? In other words, can we use this brain empowerment to unlearn or relearn to promote interdependence and advocate unity?

We can't emphasize enough both the power and the empowerment of the brain during these times of social divisiveness. The human brain is the anchor for self-reflection and self-reflection is an anchor for "crucial" thinking, especially during mindful-driven matters concerning human diversity. For resource relative to applying critical thinking between self-reflection and social issues such as human diversity, we recommend reading the work of Maureen Linker in **Intellectual Empathy: Critical Thinking for Social Justice (2014)**. Based on Linker's timely work, the author offers an applied process for not only self-reflection but a step-by-step methodology for facilitating mindful discussions about socially divisive challenges. Linker references examples for classroom discussions, social media dialogue, and diversity leadership training. Combined with our suggested taxonomy and framework for critical thinking, we believe Linker's publication would be useful for future higher educations, psychologists, and other social scientists who read this book and consider its content for future breakthrough thinking about human diversity and social unity.

The stakes are simply too high for all stakeholders across our beloved country to not respond to the ongoing, magnifying, and escalating crisis of human division and the so desperate need for engagement, enlightenment, and acceptance to human diversity. Indeed, this a serious challenge to our modern, mindful, and future civilization on Earth. The Greek philosopher *Plato* observed that the beginning is the most important work, and the Roman philosopher *Seneca the Younger* pointed out that every beginning comes from some other beginning's work. Human beings and their God-gifted brains have been around for a very, very long time (**Figures R and S),** and this essay has relevance to brains all over the world. All humans have a brain; every academic discipline needs the brain; and addressing all human challenges require brain function.

This book is about emancipating taxonomical thought leadership from within the brain to mitigate against human division and unite human diversity. Cultural evolution was a dominant force driving the human species and genetic evolution over the last few hundred thousand years (Henrich, 2011), and cultural difference in human behavior have been widely discussed, documented and interpreted by psychological theories that accentuate affective and cognitive mechanisms (Han, 2015). Among the new emanating areas about cultural changes is "culture economics" (Sundem, 2012, pg., 150). Lequerica and Krch (2014) summarized, "culture is a learned system of values, beliefs, and attitudes that is shared by a group of people …the United States is becoming increasingly diverse" (p. 645). Levitin (2015) in ***The Organized Mind*** observes, "some of the largest changes we are facing as a society are the cultural changes to our social world and the way we interact with each other" (p.120). American writer, James Baldwin once remarked, "not everything faced can be changed but everything that must change needs to be faced". With this historical and contemporary backdrop, our book is organized around a sequence of sections about the human brain, human diversity, and human division in the past, present and future American psyche (**Figure T**).

As educators, we realize that examining human diversity through and from the lens of neuroscience is exceedingly complicated and complete with cerebral and cognitive complexity. Thus, similar to the suggestion that the right brain is creative and the left is logical is an oversimplification, we recognize that connecting neuroscience to neurodiversity is also an oversimplification unless one recognizes the wide range of complexities between the two relative to mindset, values, behaviors, attitudes, and propensities. We ask our readers to join our pursuit toward narrowing the distance between science and diversity as our nation moves closer to becoming a disunited America where, according to a 2008 Pew Research Center Technical Report, non-whites are projected to be the majority here and in Europe by 2050. While we attempt to narrow this distance and close possible gaps, we welcome the relative new field of cultural neuroscience that examines the intersections between neurobiological systems and cultural environments, this new field should interest our undergraduate readers who are pursuing not only psychology or education but sociology, anthropology, and other social sciences. For students interested in emerging technology Shannon Murphy Robinson, in ***The Neuroscience of Inclusion*** **(2017)**, points out profound advances in neuroscience and technology that explore wiring of human minds.

Our book poses more questions than answers. Fundamentally, are there deeper neurological or neuroscientific phenomena between human division and human diversity that needs more in-depth proactive examination to prevent tragedies like the killing at Bowie State? Is there a relationship between mental illness, diminished capacity and racism? How might this contribute to an increasingly dividing nation? Are Americans using the highest order or highest level of cognitive empowerment and cerebral power to crucially think these tragic incidents through before, during and after they manifest? Do we think before we access or act? How will we levitate as a society and lift ourselves as human beings if we fail to proactively examine these horrific events, unsettling incidents and troubling occurrences before they happen? We believe humans are too often intellectually isolated from the cerebral benefits of neuro-socio-scientific human diversity. Imagine this type of cognitive hierarchy, metaphorically symbolized by a steep taxing tiring upward stairway.

Climbing the stairs can be increasingly tiring, uncomfortable, inconvenient, taxing, stressful, and laborious. In fact, many even think about only climbing halfway and returning to the bottom. However, by not climbing to the top, you may not seek the rewards and returns on investment from unrealized, undiscovered, underutilized and unleased neuro capacity as well as neuro capability above your shoulders, between your ears and behind your eyes. If the mid-level up the stairs meets more in-depth difficulty with a need for deeper analysis before laboring further, we suggest pulling that level out of the taxonomy, creating a new step specific to that challenge, then returning to the original taxonomy before levitating upward toward the higher order levels (or stairway steps). Toward this defining end, here is how our book is organized for our undergraduate readers.

First, we will briefly chronicle many historical events concerning human diversity challenges in America and follow these events with more recent occurrences. Before that, though, we want to point out the importance of human psychology here in the beginning. Mays and others in the ***Journal for Social Action in Counseling and Psychology*** observed, "Psychology has a body of science that can help the United States to understand why and how it creates a society that is damaging…"*Is there an issue and volume to accompany this journal other than page 12?*

(p.12). Indeed, the study of human psychology in collaboration with other related disciplines can be quite enlightening to a "thinking thoroughly throughout" experience and process for engaging in the challenges of human diversity.

Caveat #2: The Importance of Human Psychology as Science

- *The 2009 Science of Behavior Change Report (NIH) recommend an increase in support from funding agencies, including federal, non-profit, corporate, community, and university sources, for training graduate student and early career professionals for STEM-related activities in technology and other relevant disciplines.*
- *The 2004 Report to the National Science Foundation by Levine, Abler, and Rosich, Educational and Training in the Social, Behavioral, and Economics Sciences: A Plan of Action also recommended an increase in resources for the teaching of psychology as a laboratory science at the high school, community college, and college level.*
- *The 2012 STEM Vital Signs Report released by Change the Equation, data on the STEM pipeline is daunting and no state is on track to getting all students the STEM skills they need to succeed in college and careers. Low-income and minority students lag farthest behind.*
- *The 2009 Report of the American Psychology Association/ Presidential Task Force: On the Future of Psychology as a STEM Discipline (2010) also recommended that psychological science courses emphasize the critical role of psychology within the interdisciplinary science perspective.*

These national reports highlight the importance of generated psychology from the human brain. A book we recommend as complementary and companion reading for this book is ***Cross-Cultural Psychology: Critical Thinking and Contemporary Applications*** (2016) by Eric B. Shiraev and David Levy. We will try to integrate some premises from brain puissance, paradigms of crisis, and certain principles of human psychology amid our involuting world challenges. A challenging world can introduce the human mind with levitating opportunities to examine life's constant ironies, mysteries, paradoxes, and contradictions – especially relative to human diversity. Our literature review did not reveal much in terms of brain diversity in our pursued context. Much of today's research about the brain has been dedicated to autism, dementia, artificial intelligence, trauma, and other areas related to intelligence enhancement. While these areas are important to the human condition, has our dividing nation reached a point of potentially catastrophic crisis that warrants inquiry, exploration, and examination of neuro diversity? **We threaded thematic caveats throughout our book to anchor and advance a train of thought.**

Given the anticipated readership profile of our book, we recommend that readers also include "30-Second Brain: The Most Mind-Blowing Ideas in Neuroscience, Each Explained in Half A Minute" (2017) as a supplemental source to this publication. Another companion reading, specific to diversity, is contained in a collection of research narratives authored by a number of thought leaders and published as *The Latest Research Diversity by the* *Harvard Business Review* (2019). **these narratives reinforce the value of diversity in the face of creativity, problem solving and innovation.**

Proviso.#1: Potential - Possible Student Learning Outcome

After completing academic studies in neurodiversity, students will have the ability to analyze and access basic theories and applications from inquiry, exploration and examination in human diversity and neuroscience.

Second, we will attempt to make the argument for a cognitive, cerebral and "climbing" thought process that challenges the brain to hierarchically magnify, heighten and widen the mind from potentially negative and lower order thinking toward more positive and higher order thinking from already existing theoretical frameworks, perspectives and taxonomies. Many people underestimate the magnificent capacity and tremendous control of the human brain. Only when we begin to understand the brain from interdisciplinary perspectives will we be able to fully utilize its functions and realize its exponential potential. As we climb, interweave or navigate the diverse infrastructures of the brain with its collage of diverse chemical communications, we learn to appreciate the inextricable relationship of mind and body, and the levels of knowing the self through intra-psychic explorations and interpersonal relations. Exploring the neurons, wonderments, circuits, transmitters, and elements of the brain allows us to not only understand the complexities and challenges of human diversity but to also understand that which is common to all humans. As recognized by Bass in ***Social Justice Leadership for a Global World***, "The ethic of care suggests that everyone should be moved by needs, inequities, social ills, and problems faced by the other …to the ethic of community, one considers the community over individual concerns" (p. 49).

Third, we will discuss higher learning, past psychology amid perplexing phenomenon, and our institution's commitment to human diversity. Our book includes many inserts of resourceful links to readily provide data, sources, and information to our readers. Fourth, we will cover some areas related to brain matter, the brain's lobes, and other mindful matters. Fifth, we cover areas regarding crucial thought leadership, learning and logic. Sixth, we comment on areas concerning **neuroscience, neuro-diversity and neuro disorders. Seventh, we will culminate the book with some thoughts for our readers.** Our book purposefully aims to start dialogue, discourse, and discovery about what may be obvious to many but avoided by most – hopefully forcing us to look inward instead of looking outward - through the lens of psychology, cognition, mindfulness, and underleveraged brain capacity amid modern cultural neuroscience. **The 1990s was named "*The Decade of the Brain*" (Pinker, 2009). Might we revisit this decade anew, given recent dividing movements, occurrences, events, and unravelling human phenomenon? Can America's undergraduates ignite the nerve to unite?**

II.
Our History, Our Crisis, Our Brains, and Our World Challenges

Our U.S. History

Since the founding transformative origins of the United States of America, there have been many landmark events, occurrences, movements, turning watershed points, and mile-stoning metrics to help understand and accept the phenomenon of how human diversity is conceptualized as part of the "American psyche". Our most recent revelations in our history occurred in Sacramento, California and Baton Rouge, Louisiana – both capital cities in the United States. An article describing one facet of the American psyche was recently published on January 22, 2017 in the ***Chronicle of Higher Education*** (Parry, 2017). The article is called, "*Brains from Which the Alt-Right Sprang*", and we encourage our readers to examine it for a socio-historical perspective.

Our Politics

We offered a scholium on brain diversity that predates the national elections of 2008-2016, and which was presented to President Obama's White House Initiatives on Historically Black Colleges and Universities (HBCUs) in 2015 by one of the authors. In the magazine, ***INSIGHT,*** (2016) the following was reported about the White House presentation concerning:

> *Provost Joseph Martin Stevenson, Ph.D., provost and chief academic officer [for] The Chicago School [of Professional Psychology], recently presented to President Barack Obama's Board of Advisors about The Chicago School's role in addressing diversity in leadership, as well as the partnership between historically black colleges and universities... As part of his presentation to the president's board of advisors, Dr. Stevenson said, "The role of HBCUs in the U.S. provides opportunities to partner with other institutions of higher learning to advance a national agenda for embracing cultural diversity, promoting economic development, understanding the human dynamic, and advancing leadership for organizations and institutions throughout the country... in the new globally diverse economy."(pg,10)*

Interestingly, the Trump Administration, during Black History Month in 2017, issued an Executive Order to prioritize HBCUs and highlight their critical importance in the American economy. Following the above photo opportunity with President Trump and HBCU presidents, more recently, the Trump administration has suggested that funding HBCUs may be unconstitutional. Some have suggested that this threatens the central core of human diversity. http://www.politico.com/story/ 2017/05/05/trump-historically-black-colleges-financing- unconstitutional -238061. Guillermo: HBCU Funding Latest Target of White House Threats to Diversity.

The gentleman directly pictured to the left behind President Trump above was appointed in Spring of 2018 to be the chair of the HBCU advisory board for the White Initiative for HBCUs in America. There is still hope for our country's treasured HBCUs.

Other new developments for watershed points in recent very history include immigrant borders, travel bans, refugee barriers and "DACA". The nature of "isms" is transdisciplinary and rooted in social, economic, cultural and historical contexts – social events, human experiences and behavioral conditions surrounding the human mind that are onerous to change once they occur. These events have included, but are not limited to, the Native founding heritage of this country, the Civil War conflict, the Civil Rights movement, the Voter Registration Act, the Women's movement, the LGBTQ movement, the incubation and redevelopment of Affirmative Action laws, new youth movements to date, and the infusion of earlier multicultural curriculum innovations. Among the most deeply disturbing is the 13th Amendment (the abolishment of slavery and involuntary servitude, except as punishment for a crime), which still has unsettling impact and troubling implications to this day. Some research has suggested that one in three African American boys will experience imprisonment in America, and that most African American male drivers will be pulled over by the their early 20s. Sophia Kerby (2012) for the Center for American Progress in ***The Top 10 Most Startling Facts About Men of Color and Criminal Justice in the United States*** cites the following research from a look at racial disparity:

- While people of color make up about 30% of the U.S. population, they account for 60% of those imprisoned
- According to the bureau of justice statistics one in three black men can expect to go to prison during their lifetime
- Students of color face harsher punishments in school, and are more apt to be singled out for punishment than their white peers ultimately leading to a higher number of youths of color incarcerated
- According to recent data by the Department of Education African American students are arrested far more than their white classmates
- African American youths have higher rates of juvenile incarceration and are more likely to be sentenced to adult prison
- As the number of women incarcerated has increased by 800% over the last three decades, women of color have been disproportionately represented
- The war on drugs has been waged primarily in communities of color while people of color are more likely to receive higher offenses (felonies vs. misdemeanors) and once convicted black offenders receive longer sentences as compared to white offenders

- Voter laws that prohibit people with felony convictions from voting disproportionately impact men of color
- Studies have shown that people of color face disparities in wage trajectory following release from prison

We encourage the viewing of the film *13th* which is available on NETFLIX. It highlights examples for irony, contradiction, devastation, and hypocrisy.

Again, this book is about emancipating taxonomical thought leadership from within the brain to mitigate against human division and unite human diversity. Our frameworks bridge between sociological and physiological domains.

Our Crisis

Our society has also observed the creation of countless theoretical and practical frameworks for responsive public policies on social justice, the introduction of cultural diversity awareness amid intense transnationalism in the global context, emerging social media complexities as the result of "internet speak", "self-selective data", "alternate facts", "false news", "half-truths", "partial information", "fake news", "phantom fear", "fear mongering media" "phony facts", increasing provocative radio talk, widespread baseless hearsay, and other emerging communications through cyber technologies. In the televised HB0 series, "Real Time", a segment called "I Don't Know It For a Fact. . .I Just Know It Is True", characterizes this phenomenon with humor.

Authentic or not, these powerfully emotive terms – often absent of in-depth critical thought leadership – have become part of America's cultural lexicon, informal language, and common lingo -- especially in the rapidly accelerating public domain of social media. Could it be that there is a reason and rationale to suggest that the explosive emergence of social media has resulted in contributing to more social division and divide versus social unity and mutuality?

Perhaps the most recently heightened occurrence was in Charlottesville, Virginia where "both sides" were accused of igniting violence. We have also witnessed recent challenges concerning faith-based and religious orientations, modern transgender evolution, and other recent human division against human diversity challenges as the result of hyper-racially-sensitive occurrences in Oakland, Ferguson, Charleston (SC), San Bernardino, Chicago, Dallas, Orlando, Minneapolis, Baton Rouge, Charleston (WV), Cambridge (MA), Tulsa, Sacramento, Fresno, Balch Springs, and several other cities earlier in Florida as well as other venues throughout our nation in urban, rural and suburban areas (Stevenson, 2015). In American academe, many diversity challenges and related racially sensitive issues have been emerging from University of California at Davis to the University of Minnesota, to Princeton and Columbia Universities

Human division continues to mount in the South concerning the removal of confederate symbols, monuments, and statues from New Orleans, Louisiana to Charlottesville, Virginia. In another recent event in higher education, the protests at arguably the world's premier public university – the University of California, Berkeley – has received international attention and global media coverage. The below image was captured many months before the organized protest at Berkeley concerning the visit of Kellyanne Conway and suggestion of the "emboldening" of social media.

(http://thehill.com/homenews/administration/317503-conway-media-emboldened-berkeley-protesters)

Elizabeth Popham for Politics Daily (slideshow below)

Many other incidents have occurred since the election, including a truce in Sacramento and Baton Rouge, but we choose to only spend a limited time referencing them so that the readers can focus on the psychology, the brain, and neuro-scientific aspects of our book. We might add, however, as of the most recent draft (September 17, 2017) of this book, the below incident has occurred, which appears to present a pattern of behaviors that are sorrowfully chronicled in our Appendix A.

This hopefully disruptive, suppositional narrative and book is particularly relevant now, when political leaders gravitate the minds of their voting bases to human issues that only engage lower taxonomical-cognitive levels of crucial thinking. We believe the adjective "crucial" signifies, stresses, and substantiates significantly more weighted importance of the issues as exemplified by the referenced example, "infancy…is now understood as a 'crucial' building block of human personality" (www.thefreedictionary.com). The above very important historical narrative attempts to regulate, codify, dominate, control, temper, prescribe, methodize, amend, and govern human behavior have resulted in circumstances, consequences and conditions that remain disconcerting, unsettling and troubling.

However, we might understand the "isms" – and change as imperfect human beings – by unlocking internal capabilities and unleashing innermost capacities of the brain and the mind – the three-pound (*weight of the human brain*) gorilla in the room. Aamodt and Wang (2009) in ***Welcome to Your Brain,*** speculate that William James, arguably the founder of modern psychology, suggested that humans "have more mental resources than they use" (p. 7). This three-pound divine gift (**Figure Q**) that "represents about 3 percent of the body weight, but consumes around 20 percent of the body's energy, all day every day, even during sleep" (Markman and Duke, 2016) is recognized in ***Brain Briefs***. This brain-anchored topic may be so obvious to many but avoided by most – because it labels us as imperfect human beings to look (*mindfully/personally/accountably*) inward instead of looking (*relying on others and social metrics)* outward. This is also the manifestation of how people interact or do not interact. In their chapter, "*Is Prejudice Avoidable*?", Markman and Duke (2016) observe "there is a tendency for people to like other people who are like them in some way … people you spend time with end up forming an in that naturally creates an 'us' versus 'them' distinction … the solution to prejudice and dislike is diversity of interaction" (pp., 205-206). As Pettijohn and others (2008) recognized, "prejudice is a serious issue that has perpetually faced humankind". MIT Professor Alex Pentland in his work on social physics, suggest that creative group output can be modeled, tested, and improved by structuring the flow of communication between members of the group (Rosenblum, 2017). Meissner and Wulf (2016) found in their research for the ***European Management Journal*** that "group composition aspects can play an important role for improving judgement in decision-making teams and open promising new avenues for studying debiasing in behavioral strategy research".

Proviso #2

After completing group diversity-dynamic activities and exercises in class, students will have the ability to understand the challenges and competencies with group diversity and human dynamics related to gender, generation, race, religion, age, anatomy, culture, ethnicity, economics, and sexual orientation.

Is there a connection between Markman, Duke, Pentland, Meissner, and Wulf that should be considered when humans interact in groups and assigned to examine regions of the brain as related, affected and impacted by the realities of human diversity – especially if given a structured cognitive climbing process? Neuroscientist David Eagleman (2015) suggests that perception of reality is less to do about what is out there, and more to do with what is in here [the brain]. He suggests that humans need to know how the brain constructs the multisensory reality from within the "silence of the skull". This profound assessment is both metaphorically represented and metaphysically personified in the recent remarkable HBO Series, *Westworld.* What lessons could be learned from these vexing, alarming, disquieting and disturbing phenomena in Oakland, Ferguson, Charleston, San Bernardino, Chicago, Dallas, Minneapolis, Baton Rouge, Cambridge, Sacramento, Fresno, Tulsa, and others? Most recently, in Tulsa, a jury acquitted a police officer for shooting an unarmed Black man. Similar results continue to occur in other cities throughout the U.S.

https:// www.washingtonpost.com / news / morning-mix / wp / 2017 / 05/18/ tulsa – officer – acquitted – in – fatal – shooting – of – unarmed – black -man/? noredirect=on&utm_term =.a4d50a0fcef3

Regarding the "novo" (*novo* from Latin for new, compound *de novo* meaning anew) in our metaphor, we recognize Eagleman (2015) who warned, "To the brain, the future can only ever be a pale shadow of the now. The power of now explains why people make decisions that feel good in the moment but have lousy consequences in the future "(p. 119). Levitin (2014) recognizes that "every day, we are confronted with dozens of decisions, most of which we could characterize as insignificant or unimportant … for things that don't matter critically, we make a choice that satisfies us and is deemed sufficient" (p. 4). McClure (2011), professor at Stanford University adds, "…our decisions are also determined in part by how ready and willing we are to pursue and use reasoning..." (p.115) That said, since the recent U.S. Presidential election victory, there have been hundreds of reports of unrest, discrimination, violence, rallies, vandalism, threats, harassment, annoyance, dismay, and intimidation—emotively ignited by the racist, anti-foreign, sexist, classist, homophobic and other arguably offensive rhetoric. As of November 13, 2016, the Southern Poverty Law Center has received 200 hate crime reports since Election Day (http://time.com/4569129/racist-anti-semitic-incidents-donald-trump/). Moreover, many worldwide protests occurred the day of and day after the Presidential Inauguration (https://www.bloomberg.com / politics / articles / 2017 – 01 – 21 / women-s-march-draws-thousands-to-washington-to-protest-trump). If as much of voting America voted in one apparent direction before 2008, and much of voting America went the opposite apparent direction after 2016, paradigm shifts had to occur from nationwide mindful past and present experiences, amid escalating incidents between local police and Black males.

We provide highlights of some incidents, prior to 2016, concerning Black males in our enclosed Appendix A. In the city where one of the authors lives, the local Sheriff's Department was recently sued by the local ACLU office for targeting Black males and others with illegal searches, illegal seizures, and unconstitutional detention and arrests while doing nothing wrong. "Devastating" according to *The Guardian* (2017).

<https://www.theguardian.com/us-news/2017/may/08/ mississippi-african-americans-illegal-searches-aclu-lawsuit>

These real-life incidents, like those in Sacramento and Baton Rouge, could be used for the classroom group work that we will introduce later as part of our "taxonomical" advocacy for advancing "cognitive climbing". After every event, troubling incident, or disturbing occurrence from critical analysis "afterwards", there must be – to unite our dividing nation -- the crucial analysis of "beforewards" to proactively prevent the next afterwards. Were there any cognitive or cerebral lessons learned from the unfortunate succession of situations chronicled in Appendix A? With so many of these events manifesting, what have we learned?

Since the 2016 presidential election, and following the presidential inauguration, many protests occurred in major cities throughout the U.S. and around the world. The women's march the day after the inauguration was estimated as the largest in history. Early projections showed that over 2.5 million people participated in the Women's Marches around the globe (***USA Today Network,*** 2017). Although the protests, rallies, revolts, and demonstrations were primarily about gender equity issues, many others participated in this historical event to protest social injustice and human inequality. To date (September 2017), Cal Berkeley has experienced several challenges to free speech --- a tradition of this world class campus that dates back at least a half a century.

Figure A: Image of Women's March, Post 2017 Presidential Inauguration

Women's March
NY Times on the Women's March

Eagleman (2011) warns, "this built-in myth of human equality suggests that all people are equally capable of decision making, impulse control, and comprehensive consequences. While admirable, the notion is simply not true" (p.187). Might we need more exhaustive force field analyses examined between external (society) and internal (mind) variables, pressure points, intersections, forces, axis, nexus, and other oscillating/conflicting confluences– internally within and externally beyond? Kashdan (2016) suggests that "each of us holds a vested interest in how the human mind works … and interactions with the outside world is essential to living fully and improving our quality of life …to understand the mind, we must challenge conventional wisdom when appropriate"

Caveat #3: *About one of the book's metaphors*

> *"800-pound gorilla" is an English expression for a person or organization so powerful that it can act without regard to the rights of others ... The metaphor has been mixed, on occasion, with the metaphor of the elephant in the room" (Wikipedia). Elephant in the room" or "Elephant in the living room" is an English metaphorical idiom for an obvious truth that is either being ignored or going unaddressed...also applies to an obvious problem or risk no one wants to discuss (Wikipedia).*

Do we now need new valiant, audaciously courageous, and intrepid as well as inventive theories constructed amid this apparent human point that is increasingly becoming a catastrophic, profound, unprecedented public health labyrinth? In the 1970 profoundly enlightening, timeless and classical book, ***The Structure of Scientific Revolutions*** Thomas Kuhn, a pioneer in paradigm shifts, captured an essence of relevance here for our "crucial" advocacy. He writes the following in the chapter entitled, "*The Response to Crisis*":

> *"Let us then assume that crises are a necessary precondition for the emergence of novel theories and ask how scientists respond to their existence. Part of the answer, as obvious as it is important, can be discovered by noting first what scientists never do when confronted by even severe and prolonged anomalies. Though they may begin to lose faith and then to consider alternatives, they do not renounce the paradigm that has led into the crisis" (p. 77)*

Are we at this place of crisis? Might the mind and the brain need reengineered cognitive or cerebral structures to understand, embrace, and accept diversity? The World Economic Forum (www.weforum.org) recently identified the top global challenges of our times. They include areas concerning agriculture and food security; economic growth and social inclusion; environment and natural resource security; future and global financial systems; gender parity; international trade and investment; and investment in infrastructure and development. These compelling areas will be reliant from, dependent upon, and contingent with our meeting the challenges of human diversity. The early wisdom of Plato and Seneca is most relevant here, and UCLA recently announced, "The Brain: Our New Frontier" in the latest issue of the ***UCLA College Magazine*** (collegecomm@support.ucla.edu) with fascinating, edifying, and remarkable revelations about the human brain. We encourage this reading. We are quite moved by UCLA's Chancellor Gene Block, who recently reacted to the Presidential executive order imposing travel restrictions by stating, "The executive order directly challenges the core values and mission of universities to encourage the free exchange of scholars, knowledge and ideas."

Our "disruptive" challenge in this publication is to the readers of the book, and to the conference participants at the International

Conference for National Association of African American Studies and Affiliates in Dallas, Texas. Our human challenge is the following:

> ***We are now at a point of crisis and need for a human paradigm shift. It is now time to understand the dynamics of human diversity, as well as the drivers of human division, from the momentum, impetus, and genesis where this phenomenon should have been anchored from origin: the brain and the human mind – the three-pound gorilla in the room – a topic of considerable sensitivity because it requires humans to look at something inward instead of relying on something outward***

Davidson (2014) of Duke University in ***Now You See It: How the Brain Science of Attention Will Transform the Way We Live, Work, and Learn,*** captured an undergirding premise of our disruptive challenge by observing, "imagine what schools would be like today if the design work that has gone into fighter-pilot simulators and the splendid interfaces in geriatric games had gone into challenge and simulating learning games for schoolkids" (p. 156). We observe the same retrospection for the magnificent marvel and untapped prowess in neuro diversity. Henrich (2011), Research Chair in Culture, Cognition and Coevolution at the University of British Columbia, in his scientific brief for the American Psychological Association (APA) recognizes that, "neuroeconomic studies suggest that social norms are in fact internalized as intrinsic motivations in people's brains". With the vast amount of information our brains take in from the outside world, we couldn't possibly interpret it all, and to allow us to free our attention to more important matters, our brains tend to categorize our information automatically (implicitly) for quick analysis and decisions. Our brains are constantly fusilladed by incalculable sensations streaming in as we interact with our surroundings (Eliezer, 2015).

Markus (2010) at Stanford University also discerns, "to make progress in our understanding of how cultures shape brains and brains shape culture, we need to know what psychological and behavioral tendencies are associated with these social categories and how these tendencies are linked to brain function." (Lende, 2010). Indeed, examining this further is an onerous, laborious, and operose human task, especially in the current political climate and changing demographic culture. Observantly looking outward to societal protocols (rules, standards, compliance, laws, etc.), -- although undoubtedly and fundamentally necessary – is much easier, accessible, comfortable, frictionless, convenient, expeditious, low maintenance and less disruptive. Consciously looking inward focuses on the "**me**" and "**i**" in the word A**me**r**i**ca because too often we get in the way of ourselves. Hence, as pointed out in ***Change Agents*** by Debra Harris, "the three most difficult words to speak are, 'I was wrong'" (p. 128). It is more disruptive and requires self-accountability, self-reflection, strategic mindfulness, personal responsibility and ill carelessness. It also has internal biological impact to the mind and the external environmental influences in the mind's surroundings – indeed, multi-factorial. Most importantly, it requires human beings to be respectful, patient with others' ignorance, incoherence, and incompleteness.

It is human nature to implicitly deflect blame and accept praise. Human imperfection is many times misunderstood as to whether the perceived behavior is either unintentional or intentional. However, the results from the inside and internal view may empower the mind with solicitous savvy, focused judiciousness, clearer apprehension, and clarified attentiveness – especially if the empowerment is aggrandized by a structured mind-enriching taxonomy. Could not doing so could be considered some sort of indolent consciousness or a form of lethargic cognizance? Might have flight enforcement decision makers on the recent mid-April United Airlines flight applied higher order thinking and a levitated taxonomy in that situation which has ignited angst and propelled anger throughout the Asian culture in the U.S. and abroad concerning the violent removal of a 69-year-old Asian American physician? Might the law enforcement decision makers in another mid-April incident in Sacramento have applied higher order thinking from a levitated taxonomy in that situation which has ignited anger and angst among African Americans in the Sacramento community concerning the jaywalking offense by a 24-year-old African American male? How about the similar April incident involving law enforcement and the young African American male in Georgia? Understanding this human experience is high maintenance and heavy lifting for the human mind. It requires time, exhausts energy, and is exceedingly labor intensive. Consciously navigating the human mind's neurotransmissions is hard work, especially the mind that engages in respect for humanity "between" human diversity and human division.

Proviso #3

After completion of academic studies in psychology or other social science classes, students will have the ability to identify their human imperfections and compare them to those identified by their peers in class.

This requires tapping into potentially untapped cerebral sources as well as magnifying, heightening, and widening inner thoughts into outward actions. Harvard Distinguished Gardner (2007), in ***The Five Minds of the Future,*** captures some of the direction of our book in his conceptualization of the "respectful mind", defined as the awareness of and appreciation for differences among human beings. Ferraro (2015) also comments that "the path of mindfulness, awareness, kindness and compassion will take us as deep as we're willing to go". In a panel discussion at the University of Southern California, Distinguished Professor Immordino-Yang (2015) also points out that, "We first started studying emotions like compassion, emotions like admiration, inspiration ... the kinds of emotions that are the 'holy grail' in an educational context. If you can inspire teachers, if you can inspire kids and if you can design technologies and electronic ways of teaching that engage kids in ways that help them make the information part of who they are or who they want to be in the future, you have the power to change the world." (https://news.usc.edu/76466/alan-arkatov-installation-follows-education-panel/). However, Hammerness and More (2012) state that, "while the brain areas and circuits that produce emotions may be as well-ordered as a municipal power grid, we all agree emotions can be messy. Modern day neuroscience supports what is intuitive – that these emotional areas of the brain can interfere with even simple cognitive tasks" (p. 51).

How does this impact the maturing, developing and taxonomy-growing minds of children and youth?

Although the above referenced external forces like laws, policies, rules, statutes, regulations, practices, decrees, ordinances, and movements have certainly contributed to the progress and advancement of human diversity over the past decades, recent societal revelations suggest a deeper, wider and higher examination of counterinstance. There are numerous references, citations and information resources about the unrealized marvel, the unravelling mystery, and the untapped magnificence of the human brain. We identify a few here for our readers:

From: http: // www.epyk.com / 37 / 10 – interesting – facts – about - the - human-brain/

- *The human brain is the only organ in the human body that lacks nerves even though it acts as the central command for the central nervous system, through billions of neurons or "nerve cells".*
- *The human brain consumes the largest portion of the total energy that is generated in the human body. To be precise, the brain consumes 20% of that energy even though it only represents only 2% of the total body weight.*
- *The number of neurons present in the brain is approximately 100 billion which is about 15 times of the total human*

population on earth. This high number of neurons increases the processing ability of the brain.

- *The human brain is regarded as the fattest organ in the human body. About 60% of the human brain is comprised of fat which is the highest concentration of fat that is present in a single organ in a healthy human being.*
- *The neocortex is the portion of the human brain that is responsible for language and consciousness. It makes up approximately 76% of the human brain and making it the largest when compared to that in other animals.*
- *It is believed by many that, human beings use less than 10% of their brain. This is a misconception because each and every part of the brain has a known function.*
- *During early pregnancy, neurons have shown to multiply at a rate of 250,000 neurons per minute.*
- *About 15-20% (750 ml) of the total cardiac output is directed to the brain every minute.*
- *The energy consumed by the brain which is approximately 25 watts is enough to illuminate a light bulb.*
- *The human brain is not as perfect as it is thought of since in many instances it has been found to fool human beings making them to perceive things differently from the reality.*

From: http : // examinedexistence.com / 21 – interesting – facts – about - our-brain/

- *About 85% of the total weight of a human brain is the Cerebrum—the region of the brain responsible for motor control.*
- *Humans have the largest brain in terms of size ratio when compared to other creatures in the world.*
- *The adult human brain weighs nearly 1.5 kilograms (3 pounds). While it makes up only 2% of a person's weight, it consumes around 20-30% of the total energy.*
- *A brain uses approximately 20% of whole blood and oxygen flowing through the body to perform actions like yawning and intelligence.*

- *The brain consists of around 150,000 miles of the blood vessels, working perfectly in high speed.*
- *Creating neural pathways and reshaping existing neurons is called neuroplasticity. This is the brain's way to become more efficient and faster at completing tasks.*
- *Reading aloud or listening to a story being told is one of the most "cerebrally" engaging experiences a kid can have. Watching TV for 15,000 hours only generates about 30 minutes of brain activity. However, reading aloud fires up children's brains because they must use their imagination. This activity stimulates the electricity in the brain, promoting brain development by strengthening brain pathways.*
- *The first sense a human brain learns to detect is touch; however, it takes around 12 weeks to understand the complete feeling.*
- *Every time the brain is asked to revive memory, it creates many new connections within the mind. The older the memory, the more the connections are formed.*
- *Neocortex, 90% of the human brain, is one of the major and strong components in a human brain. It is responsible for providing consistent consciousness. The neocortex is divided into the temporal, occipital, frontal, and parietal lobes (which we discuss further later in the book in Section IV).*

Proviso #4

After completion of academic studies in biology or biological science class, students will have the ability to identify two to five facets of the brain that could contribute to understanding the complexity of human diversity and human division.

III.
Cognitive and Cerebral Levitation for Crucial Thought Leadership

Our "neuro diversity" book is intended to start transdisciplinary dialogue, discourse and discussion, particularly among undergraduate students, about the importance of human psychology concerning human diversity; the consideration of cognitive climbing and taxonomical mindfulness to understand (problem solve) human diversity, and the unleashing of brain empowerment to augment the phenomenon of cultural neuroscience – given the status of culture, climate and civility in the U.S and around the world. Lende (2010) defines that, "cultural neuroscience looks at how culture can shape cognition, how brains work in different settings, and the culture-dependent connections between cognition and brain function. Cultural neuroscience has emerged at the intersection of the incredible rise of neuroimaging research and decades of work in cultural psychology". We hope these transdisciplinary discussions will ignite interest in the academy to conduct the profound research and create what we are ambitiously calling now, "***Crucial Brain Diversity Theory: Cognitive Climbing***" (CBDT) through challenging the academy to propose bold new academic papers that emote controversy, possible theoretical frameworks, theoretical perspectives, stimulated hypotheses and other concerns, conditions, and circumstances, and the need to conceptualize a mindful nomenclature that could magnify, heighten and widen the scalability of inner thoughts – and, thus, manifest in more positive human actions and increase more collective interactions - relative to human diversity as we face the above mentioned challenges, changes, circumstances and consequences – perhaps now more than ever in history when our troubled country is widening more and more in its division.

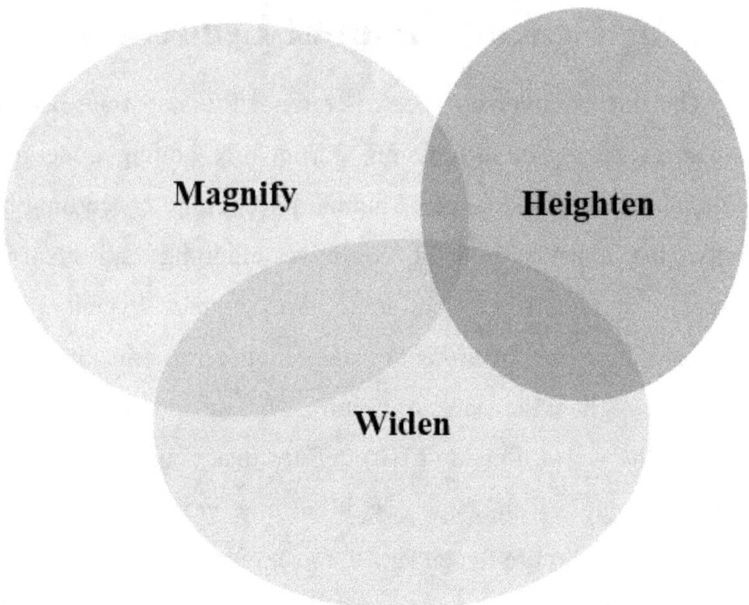

Figure B: Higher and Wider Cognition Relative to the "neuro" in our title, can racism, sexism, bigotry, misogyny, homophobia or xenophobia be unlearned from or reframed through a new defining hierarchical, multi-tier taxonomy for higher-cognitive-climbing thinking (Figure D and E)? Perhaps a paragon of cognitive climbing inclusive of the elements in Figure B for the intensifying, emerging, changing demographic audiences in Figure C?

From this admittedly arduous climbing –- perhaps as exhausting as stepping up a very high flight of steep stairs – can the rudiments of human diversity be learned, unlearned, relearned, trans-learned, reengineered? In defining diversity for our book, we reference Bianchi (2004) in **The Human Equation** for an insightful elucidation**:**

> *"Diversity includes all characteristics and experiences that define each of us as individuals. We are all influenced by who we are and where we've been. So, diversity is the differences in each of us. "Not everyone thinks of diversity in the same way. Attitudes and opinions vary widely about diversity and how it functions in the workplace, in a community, and in the world. A common misunderstanding about diversity is that only certain persons or groups are included. In truth, each and every attribute of an individual is encompassed in diversity. Everyone has a unique perspective that is defined and shaped by many experiences and influences".*

Figure C: Multi-Faceted Faces of Human Diversity

Caveat #4: *"Everything faced cannot be changed, but everything that must change needs to be faced "*

- James Baldwin

Figure D: Definition of Cognition

cog· ni· tion

[ˌkägˈniSH(ə)n]

the mental action or process of acquiring knowledge and understanding through thought, experience, and the senses. Synonyms: perception discernment apprehension learning a result of this; a perception, sensation, notion, or intuition. Synonyms: perception · discernment apprehension learning (Wikipedia).

Figure E: Definition of Climbing

climb· ing

[ˈklīmiNG]

the sport or activity of ascending mountains or cliffs. Climbing is the activity of using one's hands, feet, or any other part of the body to ascend a steep object. It is done recreationally, competitively, in trades that rely on it, and in emergency rescue and military operations. It is done indoors and out, on natural and manmade structures (Wikipedia).

Frame (2013) suggests that "our perceptions of the world are intermediated by the brain.

What we see, hear, and feel is not what we get" (p. 256). Can the neurons and networks within the brain be stimulated to create new paradigms, alternative modelling, inventive patterns or proactive actions that drive behavior? For example, visual images, taken in through our eyes, and interpreted as expressions of human anger may result in repulsion. Is it possible to interpret anguish or agony in ways that repulse negative behavior or attitude and – instead–cultivate positive behavior or attitude toward unity versus human division?

This calls for a new definition of "thought leadership". We propose this fundamental humanitarian question and another series of probing questions to think about for purposes of intellectual discourse, not to necessarily seek empirical evidence for now – until the appropriate research questions are framed with conceptual frameworks to position inquiry for empirically-based research for evidence seeking. To do this, we need the climbing "levitation" to navigate the mindful maze (**Figure F, G and H**). We attempt to note this in our sub-title relative to desperately needed "higher" ***and*** "wider" order thought leadership across diverse America.

Figure F: Human Connections Within the Mind

Caveat #5: *"At the end of the day, we are all connected." Howard in "Collateral Beauty"*

Siegel (2017) recognizes that "in our journeys through life, unexpected turning points arise, and we often do not understand their long-term impact" (p.140). This book is a starting point of labyrinth to a very intricate, complex, entangled, and complicated journey that will be complete with mazes, obscurity, and oscillating perspectives from psychological, social, ideological and biological lens. We want to build past knowledge bases, revelations in the present literature, contemporary constructs in the global academy, voids or gaps in the research, and emerging global conversations about human diversity – and human division – at arguably a most crucial time in history. We realize that our book poses more questions than answers. We deeply believe this is fundamental to the leveraging of the brain for resolve. Indeed, in this regard, brainstorming is one way of achieving resolution.

As noted in March – April 2018 issue of Harvard Business Review, (HBR.ORG) "Brainstorming for questions rather than answers makes it easier to push past biases and venture into unchartered territory" (p. 67). Perhaps our resolve is not palpable by policy anchored effects from external society; but from personally internal effects and affects from the mind that is manifested and evinced in positive changed behavior, upward climbing cognition, changed attitude, transferred dispositions, modified deportments, altered comportment, disrupted complacency, or renewed cognizance. To do this, we ladder upwards with steps for cognitive climbing. Three good examples on how the mind and brain neurons can be navigated to conceptualized thinking patterns or paragons is evidenced in both our K-12 and postsecondary systems. For at least the past 60 years, the American K-12 system has employed Bloom's taxonomy of educational objectives (**Figure G2)** as the cognitive-rising rubric for moving the thinking process among children and youth from lower order thinking to higher order based on increasingly elevated levels of crucial thinking and active learning.

Proviso #5

After completion of academic studies in social science or humanities, students will have the ability to identify a framework for elevating from a lower level in a taxonomy to a higher level to understand some challenge, condition, circumstance or consequence concerning human diversity or human division.

Ugur, Constantinescu and Stevens (2015) in the *Eurasian Journal of Educational Research,* demonstrated how Bloom's Taxonomy "provides the architecture needed to implement self-determination theory in such a way that students are able to engage in a programmatic process of self-development" (p. 90). They go on to conclude, "The process of self-development can be facilitated by the internalization of cognitive learning and is supported by affective processes that, together, yield favorable developmental outcomes for students…" (p. 90). In this era of heightened emotive sensitivity about human diversity in an environment of widening use of everyday analytics and overwhelming informatics, a structural methodology for hierarchical thought process could prove prudent in self-development, problem solving, conflict resolution, mindful reasoning, and other crucial thinking. Firestien (2017) provides some cautionary observations that should be considered for the process of problem solving in *The Power of Incubation*. He writes,

> *"When your brain is at rest or you do not feel psychologically threatened you are at your most creative. Some think it is because when your brain has been uninterrupted, it gives it time to refresh itself. You can spend too much time exploring solutions, focusing on the problem, looking at it from different angles. Your brain becomes overloaded with possibilities, complications, and the twisting and turning actually hinders your creative process. Overthinking serves as a roadblock to letting your brain work out the problem ..."*

Over two decades ago, Paul and Elder (1997) have provided fascinating frameworks for crucial thinking based on what psychologists typically call "probing", which the authors captured in the "Socratic teaching" method. Either students or the faculty could play the role of the "Socratic Questioner". What follows is an excerpt from their resourceful and enlightening website:

> *"The oldest, and still the most powerful, teaching tactic for fostering critical thinking is Socratic teaching. In Socratic teaching we focus on giving students questions, not answers. We model an inquiring, probing mind by continually probing into the subject with questions. Fortunately, the abilities we gain by focusing on the elements of reasoning in a disciplined and self-*

assessing way, and the logical relationships that result from such disciplined thought, prepare us for Socratic questioning. Thankfully, there is a predictable set of relationships that hold for all subjects and disciplines. This is given in the general logic of reasoning, since every subject has been developed by those who had:

shared goals and objectives (which defined the subject focus)
shared questions and problems (whose solution they pursued)
shared information and data (which they used as an empirical basis)
shared modes of interpreting or judging that information
shared specialized concepts and ideas (which they used to help them organize their data)
shared key assumptions (that gave them a basis from which to collectively begin)
a shared point of view (which enabled them to pursue common goals from a common framework)

Each of the elements represents a dimension into which one can delve in questioning a person. We can question goals and purposes. We can probe into the nature of the question, problem, or issue that is on the floor. We can inquire into whether we have relevant data and information. We can consider alternative interpretations of the data and information. We can analyze key concepts and ideas. We can question assumptions being made. We can ask students to trace out the implications and consequences of what they are saying. We can consider alternative points of view. These, and more, are the proper focus of the Socratic questioner. As a tactic and approach, Socratic questioning is a highly-disciplined process. The Socratic questioner acts as the logical equivalent of the inner critical voice which the mind develops when it develops critical thinking abilities. The contributions from the members of the class are like so many thoughts in the mind. All the thoughts must be dealt with and they must be dealt with carefully and fairly. By following up all answers with further questions, and by selecting questions which advance the discussion, the Socratic questioner forces the class to think in a disciplined, intellectually responsible manner, while yet continually aiding the students by posing facilitating questions.

A Socratic questioner should:
***a)** keep the discussion focused*
***b)** keep the discussion intellectually responsible*
***c)** stimulate the discussion with probing questions*
***d)** periodically summarize what has and what has not been dealt with and/or resolved*
***e)** draw as many students as possible into the discussion". (FROM:* www.criticalthinking.org*):*

Our readers should also refer to **Figure P** for alternative guidance. Hall (2005) captured the scope of this taxonomy in stating that Bloom's taxonomy as "affective learning objectives … central to learning as the cognitive objectives. These objectives begin with receiving (paying attention) and proceed through responding and valuing to organizing (conceptualizing values), culminating in characterizing (generalizing values to behavior). Though affective learning or attention to the emotional part of learning has been undervalued in educational systems, it represents a part of learning that is becoming increasingly recognized as vital" (p. 8) We encourage our readers to read about the growing global conversations here concerning "neuromyth", related neuroscience, and learning styles among human beings:

https: // www.theguardian.com / education / 2017 / mar / 13 / teachers -neuromyth-learning-styles-scientists-neuroscience-education

Another way of considering this type of process is through another process encouraged by Psychologist Robert Bjork at the University of California at Los Angeles (UCLA) called "interweaving" and "mastering one thing before moving to the next". Bjork's process appears to be more horizontal versus Bloom's vertical domains, yet upward like multi-level spiraling staircase (**Figure G1**). Bjork states (Sundem, 2012), "if information is studied so that it can be interpreted in relation to other things in memory, learning is much more powerful" (p.10). While we believe Bjork's, proposition is worth investigating toward our premises, we have elected to focus on Bloom's theoretical frame. This book advocates the enlightening, leveraging and engaging of upward thinking taxonomies for positive change and altered human behavior toward human diversity.

Figure G1: Elevating/Interweaving/Spiraling?

Figure G2: Bloom's Taxonomy of Educational Objectives (Prototype)

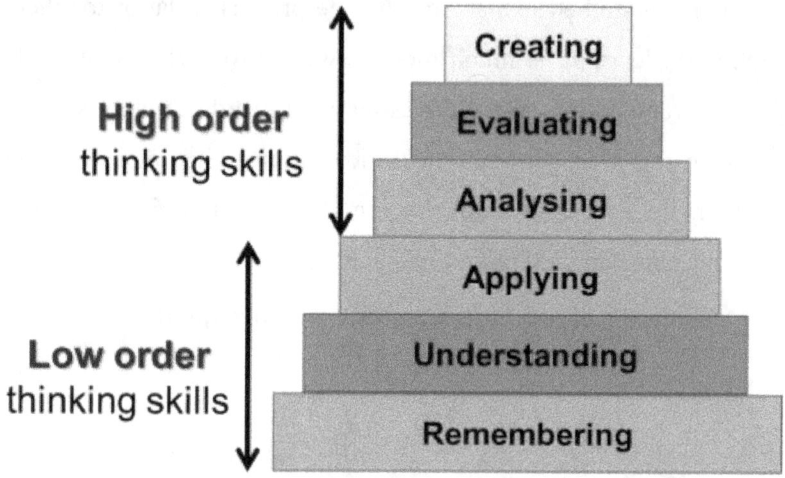

Caveat #6: *"Imagine what schools would be like today if the design work that has gone into fighter-pilot simulators and the splendid interfaces in geriatric games had gone into challenge and simulating learning games for schoolkids?"*

— Vice Provost Cathy Davidson, Duke University

The upward-elevating (and multi-tier-climbing) cognitive domains in this hierarchal rubric generally includes application, analysis, synthesis, and evaluation. Based on the work in the book, ***THEORRY*** (2015) Stevenson, Wilson and others are working on a conceptual framework that leverages the five senses toward a taxonomic hierarchy with the bottom pyramid capturing "cognizance", and the upward levels of domains advancing to "application", then "integration", then "reapplication", then "elevation", then "re-creation" of new enlightened cognizance. We believe this is the crucial thought leadership process.

In a classroom setting, students could be divided into groups by each of the five senses and conceptualize their own hierarchies by beginning with other groups' re-creations, thus developing a snowball

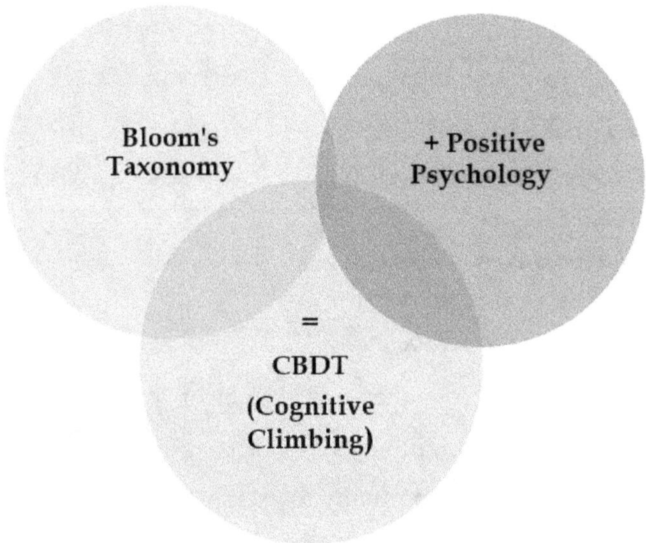

effect. This process is bound to capture rich, broad, deep, and diverse human experiences for eclectic "crucial" thought processes. In the meantime, in Bloom's theoretical and applied framework, psychomotor domain covers perception, set, guided response, mechanism, complex overt response, adaption and origination.

Modifications to Bloom's taxonomy have been made over the years but the core elements have remained constant. Student groups might also explore relationships to conventional or traditional theoretical frameworks. In addition to the numerous frameworks or perspectives in modern neuroscience, other frameworks for contextual purposes of this book could include:

- *Complexity theory**
- *Trait theory*
- *Situational theory*
- *Behavioral theory*
- *Developmental theory*
- *Cognitive theory*

- *Queer theory*
- *Feminist theory*
- *Race theory*
- *Relational theory*
- *Intersubjectivity theory*
- *Gender theory*
- *Change theory*
- *Identity formation theory*
- *Transformational theory*

Could such taxonomies and frameworks, if augmented by our paragon, be recreated for building vertical constructs in brain diversity? If students were given the opportunity to establish their own brain diversity taxonomies – with the tiers of basic knowledge or cognizance toward the bottom of the hierarchy – and advancing top tiers for recreating that knowledge from magnifying, heightening and widening the thought **(Figure H: New Cognitive Climbing for CBDT)** process – could we than suggest that Bloom's taxonomy or others could be utilized for conceptualizing a new theoretical framework and problem-solving during this time of crisis between human diversity and human division? We note here that Albert Einstein once remarked about problem-solving, "I would spend the first fifty-five minutes identifying the problem and the last five minutes solving it" (Firestien, 2017).

Proviso #6

After completion of academic studies in lower division undergraduate studies before matriculating to the upper division, students will have the ability to identify a proven empirically-based theory and apply its elements to a real-life, relevant situation, challenge, or condition concerning human diversity or human division.

Bloom's Taxonomy, and its many reconfigurations based on local school needs and school district demands, has been widely applied in public schools, private schools, faith-based school, charter schools, and other school settings throughout America, as well as abroad. Imagine the above graph of the colorful hierarchy with the left side for lower to higher order thinking remaining, but an addition of the right side with a scale that ranges from negative psychology at the bottom and positive psychology toward the top of the hierarchy. Could Bloom's taxonomy, combined with those levitating-guiding principles introduced by theorists in positive psychology be reengineered into a plausible, feasible and pragmatic framework for moving a mindful thought process from: (a) negative, lower order denomination of crucial thought to (b) positive, higher order denomination of crucial thought amid left to right; right to left brain regions, circuits, networks, faculties and neurons?

What if the right or left side of the pyramid added an upward/downward scale from like: subjective to objective; invalid to valid; inaccurate to accurate; unvetted to vetted; "biased to unbiased"; illogical to logical; pessimistic to optimistic; uncomfortable to comfortable; low maintenance to high maintenance; less labor intensive to more labor intensive; unverified to verified; incomplete to complete or others generated from some the probing questions later introduced in **Figure P.** Regarding bias in artificial intelligence, Devlin (2017) with ***The Guardian*** recently reported that "machine learning algorithms are picking up deeply ingrained race and gender prejudices concealed within the patterns of language use". How does this impact the maturing minds of children?

https://www.theguardian.com/technology/2017/apr/13/ai--programs-exibit-racist-and-sexist-biases-research-reveals

Figure I: Child Cognition with Computer Informatics

Caveat #7: *"Think left and think right and think low and think high. Oh, the thinks you can think up if only you try "*

– Dr. Seuss

Harland (2014) observes that the culture surrounding video games immense change over the past decade and "the data make it clear that gamers themselves come from a broad range of backgrounds that cover different generations, races, ethnicities and cultures". In this broadening era of the use of video games to stimulate learning among children, Case Western Reserve Professor Sandra Russ (2016) in ***THINK*** advocates that "challenging games require problem-solving techniques that actually spur creativity". To boost the creativity in children, she recommended that parents "expose them to scientific and artistic creative experiences". Distinguished Professor Russ, along with University Psychological Services Professor Louis D. Beaumont, have spent nearly three decades studying how child play relates to imagination and emotions. However, Anonymous in

The Guardian (2014) suggests:

"There's been a lot of chat lately about why people might stop playing games – in particular why little girls who grew up with consoles don't seem to stick with the hobby as they get older...Most of the time when we discuss why girls don't play

> *games it often boils down to representation: there still aren't as many female characters to relate to. For the past few years, this situation has been improving: titles such as Mirror's Edge: Catalyst, Horizon: Zero Dawn, Dishonored 2 and ReCore all have women front and centre and are all either out now or on the way. Obviously, that's great – having more female characters in games is a step forward. But to be honest I think we need to ask a different question. The problem of marginalisation in games development isn't just about women, or people from different religious or ethnic backgrounds, it's about entire genres. Marginalization is happening in the very fabric of the design process, and this is just as damaging to the health of the industry and its ability to hold our attention – both as developers and as gamers".*

These are very insightful observations concerning the digital influences of video gaming among children and youth (**Figure I**), and the potential power of embedding crucial thinking regarding human diversity at an early age within an entertainment subtext. And, although the Department of Labor six years ago speculated that 65 percent of children entering grade school in 2010 will end up working in careers (many that will be digitally and video-tech related) that haven't even been invented yet, all children must be equipped, engaged, enlightened and empowered with an early sustainable lifelong understanding of human diversity in the mind, at home, at school, at work, in the community, and in their future journeys throughout the world. Might this much-needed and life-required neuro-empowerment begin prior to elementary, middle, and high schools with elevating-sequential crucial thought taxonomies?

Higher education also employs similar problem-solving and imagination-sparking constructs through a myriad of "critical thinking" curriculum and instructional frameworks in both undergraduate and graduate education. Davidson (2011) reported that when Duke University gave out iPods to incoming freshman, there were many critics calling it "a waste" – but the university later found that the students had mindfully integrated the devices in every discipline. In American law schools, the universally applied framework for developing "thinking-like-a-lawyer-skills" is crafted within most and if not all law schools from the Socratic teaching method, which increasingly ignites and stimulates thinking order among law students from case studies, lectures, black letter law, moot court simulations, and law library.

The result of this working paradigm is not only the manifestation of a universal language and lexicon, but a common denominating framework for understanding legal principles from a taxonomical rubric for thinking through facts, issues, analysis called "IRAC", which stands for issue, rule, application conclusion and facts. Why couldn't similar cognitive rubrics, inclining taxonomies, formulating frameworks, or even digital apps for mobile devices be generated for higher order as well as wider order to support crucial brain diversity theory from thought leaders within the academy and, resultantly, challenging academic white papers that emote controversy, possible theoretical frameworks, theoretical perspectives, stimulated hypotheses and other concerns, conditions, circumstances, and challenges? Could the visual-stimulating video technology advocated for promoting imagination and creativity among children be applied for sparking understanding of human diversity? Would this not be ideologically parallel to the consistency of most, if not all school district, college and university mission statements with the embedded core values that uphold, embrace, and promulgate human diversity and mindful inclusion? Might the new global academy be vindicated as both the problem and the solution? How can undergraduate and graduate students help to solve programs and research alternative solutions and resolutions?

We propose these fundamental and other probing questions to think about for purposes of intellectual discourse until appropriate research questions are framed with conceptual frameworks to position mindful inquiry for empirical research based on substantiated evidence. Perhaps this could be generated in parallel from principled attributes and assets of positive psychology (**Figure J**) and upward domains of Bloom's taxonomy of educational objectives? Positive psychology has an intriguing history. It began with the disease model in the second half of the 19th century; then the B.F. Skinner's model of behaviorism; then the humanistic model introduced by Abraham Maslow and Carl Rogers; then the positive psychology model by Martin Seligman during his presidency of the American Psychological Association (*Positive Psychology Program Your One-Stop Positive Psychology Resource).*

Figure J: Attributes and Assets of Positive Psychology

Caveat #8: *"You see things; and you say, why? But I dream things and I say, why not?"*

- George Bernard Shaw

IV.
Higher Learning, Past Psychology Amid Perplexing Phenomenon

Higher education enterprise must continue to be committed to providing its students, faculty, staff, and surrounding community with meaningful educational experiences that focus on some human experiences from fostered understanding of human diversity, cultural difference and social division (**Figure L**). There will always be a need for a thoughtful, cerebral and cognitive process to understand of the complexities, conditions and challenges of everyday human diversity against division, and the acquisition of comprehending some of the human dynamics in our increasingly interdependent diversity-destined global economy for greatest of good.

Caveat #9: "We make the same human mistakes, and here we all are"

– Dr. Ford in "Westworld"

This book is about emancipating taxonomical thought leadership from within the brain to mitigate against human division and unite human diversity. The intersections of mindful discussions, to generate thoughtful processes, could center around the below changes, conditions, circumstances and consequences (Stevenson and Leahy,

2015) that transverse between external social forces and internal cerebral capacities (**Figure L**). These forces and counterforces were presented to psychology, law, education, leadership, and health faculty who attended a system wide retreat on teaching agents of change for social justice.

Figure L: The "Great Again America" We Live In

- *Growing, emerging and intensifying multiculturalism, confluences, trans-nationalism, internationalism, technology and geo-climate-cultural change --- locally, regionally and globally – heighten emotion from confusing and conflicting messages or media about borders, barriers, bans, and boundaries relative to immigrants, migrants and refugees;*
- *Expanding disparity and divide between the poor and the rich, resulting in higher population growth among the underserved, marginalized, impoverished, underrepresented, underutilized, underprivileged, and the oppressed peoples who want, deserve and need human justice (see the annotated bibliography for information);*
- *Residuals, results and impact from privately funded academies and publicly funded schools often characterized by racial composition, economic status and conflicting ideologies and clashing idealism about "what is an educated person?";*
- *Recession related hardships, economic downturn, employment decline, financial crises, fiscal constraints, national disasters, stress on families, and pressure on organizations and institutions, resulting in growing traumatic concern for future generations;*
- *Changing mores for a societal continuum that ranges from ultra-conservative/restrictive voices to ultra-liberal/ permissive voices with religious and political beliefs that live side by side and must, out of necessity, understand, accept, compromise, and tolerate extreme differences;*

- *Unresolved, unraveling and unrevealing historical and human feelings about race, racism and racial relations, compounded by calamitous attitudes on campus and the community about "the way we do things around here";*
- *Growing concerns about life "space-station-stage", national security, self-preservation, turfism, gentrification, individualism, territorialism, domestic immigration, personal alienation, religious conflict, amid unpreparedness for and uneasiness with accelerating globalization;*
- *Citizen discontent, frustration, impulse and inability to control or have impact upon government, educational and corporate decision-making, efficiency, ethics and corruption;*
- *Expanding voice, participation and power of women and ethnic minorities; declining voice, participation, and power of many white males; dramatic shifts in demography;*
- *Divisive discourse about public policy concerning taxation, healthcare, entitlements, rights and privileges compounded by cultural clashes about values, virtue, rectitude, probity, and morality resulting in declining patience for human imperfection and compromising regard for human compassion, human rights, and human justice;*
- *Diminishing respect for freedom of expression with accepted common decency and regard for human dignity and revering civility; ambiguity about "the purpose of higher learning for a greater good";*
- *Habitual human behavior and deportment – concerning judgments, ambiguity, perceptions, and opinions – based on unvetted verification and ignited emotionalism versus facts, analysis, evidence, data driven decision making and crucially "thinking things through thoroughly throughout";*
- *Resentment and resistance to socio-progressive change, and older intergenerational influences on younger generations that may or may not have influence, compounded by digital distractions resulting in high tech versus high touch;*

- *Remaining and resurfacing repressed human feelings from those who hold on to the Old Deep South (Post Civil War) and others to the New Deep South (Post Civil Rights); continued lock into the inherent, destructive, malign, virulent and pestilent "either/or" behavioral paradigm and cognitive mindset;*
- *Decreasing confidence in the American Dream and increasing incidents of human behaviors based on overreactions to events, insensitive reactions to events, sporadic impulses, vulnerable feelings, and episodic emotionalism; and*
- *Fear of losing perceived freedoms, rights, privileges, and entitlements; fear of losing place and position in society; fear of losing historical identity; fear of losing the ability to make choices and have alternatives based on self-comfort, convenience, complacency, personal security/safety, the pursuit of happiness; and fear of the unknow" (pp., 10-12).*

Most American colleges and universities in America have academic programs in psychology and related behavioral sciences – including public health. We ask the faculty and students affiliated with these programs to join this discourse and help to build a national community of practice with psychology, neuroscience and brain theory at the center of focus. We ask if perhaps diversity cognition should be measured or evidenced by a targeted outcome like a developed competency, a gained knowledge acquisition, a changed attitude, a new disposition, a new skill set, a new untapped awareness, etc. Perhaps beyond the institutional outcomes that are common, conventional and traditional for the accreditation, approval, or licensure of psychology programs but rather targeted climbing outcomes that are related to understanding or preventing the disturbing incidents referenced above.

Proviso #7

After completion of academic studies in the upper division undergraduate studies, students will have the ability to identify a driving force and a counterforce impact the influence of the human brain and the external environment that surrounds human behavior concerning diversity and inclusion.

Could these outcomes manifest at a social gathering – like a restaurant, workplace environment, or a place of worship – as a microcosm of the college classroom, career workplace or community neighborhood? We attempt in our book to discuss ways to bridge the internal power of the cerebral brain with the internalized empowerment from crucial thinking to confront external pressure points. All institutional sectors and organizational segments of our global society are challenged by the complexities of human diversity in the workplace, in the home place, in communities, and other settings throughout the troubling, broken, unsettling and disturbing world. Such is the case for the sectors of business, industry, education, technology, commerce, health, and all forms of government at the local, state, and federal levels. How can faculty as engaged clinical professionals, and students as prospective mental health professionals, empower individual clients and community constituencies to navigate the magnification of higher order and wider order thought leadership upward, forward and toward affirmation – or at least the acknowledgment of fundamentals for modern human diversity?

The extent to which higher education should respond, react, relate and help to resolve is a social imperative by mindfully empowering next generation leaders throughout the country with an understanding of the cerebral capacity relationships to gender, race, age, culture, class, ethnicity, and sexual orientation (GRACE, defined later in two dimensions) from everyday human situations that are relevant, real life and realistic. The higher purpose role of higher education in the United States should be to advance a national conversation for embracing cultural diversity, promoting intellectual development, understanding the human dynamic, and advancing leadership for organizations and institutions throughout the country from crucial thinking that is manifested for higher learning. Pinker (2016) points out that surveys of ethnographic studies reveal that people all over the world share an astonishing universal psychology. We can look to our shared evolutionary history to see the similarities.

We want to put out into the vast universe – that surrounds the mind and the brain – a clarion call for more research about human diversity in these most trying, very troublesome and increasingly troubling times. As advocates, proponents and enthusiasts for the study of psychology, we ask both students and faculty to identify ways to build on the past and present theoretical foundations – and help to build bold new crucial-taxonomical frameworks – from those evidence based anchored by previous psychologists from Adler's work on understanding human nature and Berne's work on human relationships; to Cialdini's work on persuasion and Csikszentmihalyi's work on invention; to Erikson's work on psychoanalysis and Eysenck's work on personality; to Anna Freud 's work on the ego and Sigmund Freud's work on dreams; to James's work on founding psychological principles and emotions to Jung's work on unconsciousness; to Gilbert's work on happiness and Gladwell's work on the power of thinking; to Maslow's work on motivation and Milgram's work on authority; to Pavlov's work on the cerebral cortex and unconscious learning and Piaget's work on thought and language; to Skinner's work on behavior and Schwartz's work on the paradox of choice; and from the work of Stone, Patton, and Heen on difficult conversations (Butler-Bowdon, 2015).

Students studying psychology might also consider Sundem's (2012) ***Brain Trust: 93 Top Scientists***. Perhaps the work by Harvard's Howard Gardner in ***Frames of Mind: The Theory of Multiple Intelligences*** (1993), ignited widespread conversations about this general topic from the perspectives of varying intelligences – linguistic, musical, logical, spatial, kinesthetic, and other applications. Gardner observed the following that may have timely relevance to how the internal mind interacts with external social media, societal images and other visuals or optics from recent events and subsequent widespread rhetoric:

> *"Much of what is distinctive about human cognition and information processing involves the deployment of various symbol systems. It is at least an open question, , an empirical issue, whether operation of one symbol system such as language involves the same abilities and processes as such cognate systems as music, gesture, mathematics, or pictures. It is equally open whether information encountered in one medium (say , film) is the 'same' as information when transmitted by another medium (say, books)" (p. 25)*

As recognized in the Chicago School of Professional Psychology's ***No Health Without Mental Health Report*** (2016), "preoccupation with social media to the exclusion of other relationships can create difficulties for some – but these networks can also be used to support and monitor those who struggle with social connection…" (p.52). Data scientist Eichstaedt (2016) who is pursuing a PhD in psychology with the University of Pennsylvania found that "the language people use in tweets and Facebook posts can indicate their age, gender, personality, income, mental state and physical health" (p. 64). What are the implications here regarding human sameness, similarity and uniqueness? Makin (2016) recently suggested that "we all suspect we're unique, and methods for identifying whether by examining fingerprints or strands of DNA, confirm this conviction". Citing a study by Emily Finn (year of publication, and you should cite the Finn study in the references) at Yale University, she reports "a recent study shows that each person's mind also exhibits a distinct pattern that could be used as a distinguishing feature with near-perfect accuracy" (p. 22).

Leveraging the metaphor behind *BEFOREWARDS*, what lessons could be learned from brain diversity as related to the above cited unsettling, alarming and disturbing videos concerning human conflict and confrontation? After all, the intentions of *BEFOREWARDS* is to inquire, investigate, and inspect how many of the disturbing incidents that society is now experiencing can be explored through the lens of psychology, related behavioral sciences and other transdisciplinary blends in higher education. We advocate the proactive need to both broaden, re-examine and modernize these general topics in response to contemporary conversations regarding human diversity dynamics, untapped human potential from the human brain, thinking about thinking and learning differently, and addressing these topics by shifting our paradigms from past experiences to present day ones – resulting in reflective cerebral bridges (from past to present) for confronting diversity. As pointed by Mary Helen Immordino-Yang in ***Emotions, Learning and Brain: Exploring the Educational Implications of Affective Neuroscience***

(2016), cognitive and emotional processes are carried out not in a vacuum, but in social, historical and cultural contexts.

Why couldn't newly developed cognitive rubrics, inclining taxonomies or formulating frameworks be generated for higher order as well as wider order to support crucial brain diversity theory through social, historical and cultural contexts to emote controversy, possible theoretical frameworks, alternative theoretical perspectives, stimulated hypotheses and other generated constructs from the below human gift? Could students in a class be into divided ***brain***storming groups – with each group assigned a lobe to concentrate on – and develop a lower to higher neuro taxonomy for crucial thinking based on an assigned human diversity case, challenge, condition, or circumstance – especially if the situation is particularly personal – and particularly in instances where there is either conflicting or contrasting mystery, contradiction, irony or hypocrisy.

It is our hope that this brainstorming experience could one day be developed into a global "virtual simulation" to provide opportunities to innovate and create or recreate their own learning experiences with others around the world. Could not students and faculty learn from these experimental/experiential encounters from leveraging the cerebral prowess in **Figure M**? For instance, many students would argue that some human stereotypes are accurate, but couldn't a cognitive structure of higher and wider order of crucial thought process suggest that all stereotypes are indeed "incomplete"? Here we encourage the process of "generative learning" defined by Verna Allee (2003) as "value -added learning that seeks what is, compelling, and energizing and that expresses a willingness to see radical possibilities beyond the boundaries of current thinking".

Proviso #8

After completion of academic studies regarding group work and team-building, students will have the ability to describe the benefits and risks with brainstorming and capturing both intellectual and cultural diversity.

Among many attributes relative to brain diversity, generative learning leverages existing knowledge, while leveraging new ideas, and empowers the human mind to recognize information and data. This is crucial in recognition of what we covered in Section II regarding "emerging social media complexities". Also, crucial to group and individual reflection concerning race, racism and race relations is another very relevant term by Allee, called "complexity theory", which "refers to the interdisciplinary exploration of a set of theories from different fields, all of which share focus on complex adaptive systems and evolution" (possible other theories are highlighted earlier on page 36).

Perhaps faculty and students could examine this type thought leadership process by considering the suggested steps and framed guidelines in Appendix B for group work in the classroom. We note, though, the context, content, and construction of the final syllabus should be left up to the creativity of the students and the faculty. Our syllabus supplement could easily be integrated in any psychology or related behavioral/social science course in higher education. For classroom instruction, our book aims to start dialogue, discourse and discovery about what may be obvious to many but avoided by most – because its forces us to look inward instead of looking outward - through the lens of psychology, cognition, mindfulness, and underleveraged brain capacity amid modern cultural neuroscience – particularly now in this post national election time of the widespread amplification of ambiguity, angst, ambivalence, and anger. However, navigating the human mind requires humans to look less outward and look more inward. The college classroom is an excellent venue for this.

Caveat #10: "I am trying to fix my mind"

– Howard in "Collateral Beauty"

Figure M: Lobes of the Human Brain

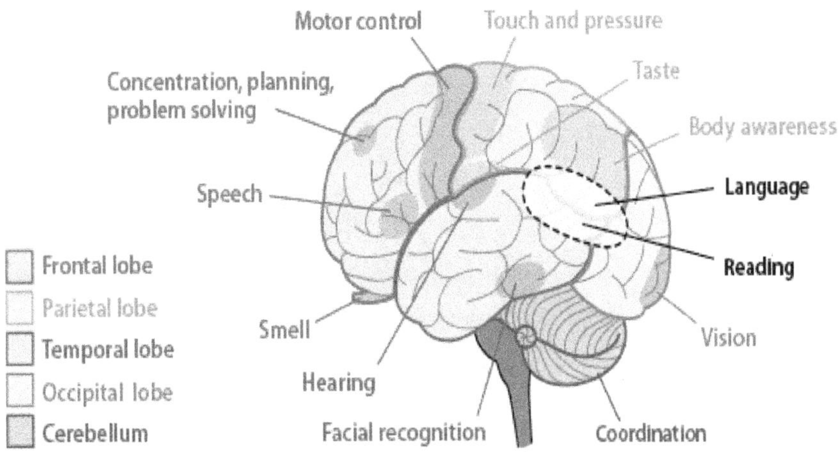

(https://askabiologist.asu.edu/what-your-brain-doing)

V.
Brain Matter, Leadership Lobes, and Other Mindful Matters

Where we would be now as a society had we – in the beginning -- approached, accepted, and "anchored" human diversity as mindful phenomenon with untapped neural capability, unrealized cognitive capability and openings for crucial thought leadership? This book is about emancipating taxonomical thought leadership from within the brain to mitigate against human division and unite human diversity. The above graphic not only denotes the power of the brain, it also displays the diverse regions of the brain that guide human thought and behavior. Davidson (2014) recognized that "how we use the brain (what we pay attention to) changes our human brain. Those things that most capture our attention – our learning and our work, our passions and our activities – change our actual brain biology" (p. 15).

Not everyone in the field knows specifically what they are (and at UCLA they were discovered as Jennifer Aniston cells, based on a specific study using the 'Friends' star). This is what I would say regarding them: In the frontal lobe of the brain, there are a group of cells that seem to respond specifically when we observe others and especially when we try to imitate or copy what others do. These cells were labeled as mirror neurons, and seem to be heavily involved in empathy responses, but may also play a role in the opposite response. About a decade ago, ***Scientific Daily*** with UCLA made the following observation to illustrate our point:

> *"The brain's mirror neuron network responds differently depending on whether we are looking at someone who shares our culture, or someone who doesn't. A thumb's up for "I'm good." The rubbing of a pointed forefinger at another for "shame on you. The infamous and ubiquitous middle finger salute for--well, you know. Such gestures that convey meaning without speech are used and recognized by nearly everyone in our society, but to someone from a foreign country, they may be incomprehensible."*

As we think about this observation and bridging the power of the brain (**Figure M**) to crucial thought relative to human diversity, there are several assumptions that can be made, and are useful here. The Frontal lobe, which controls movement of the body, the ability to problem solve, speech, and develop emotional reactions would be a region of the brain to leverage when students are crucially looking at video to discern human behavior and identify elements of diversity that would be useful to their learning. For instance, students who view the video of the past incident in Minneapolis, or the more recent occurrence in Cambridge (MA) would certainly develop emotion around the viewing and make specific connections to their own personal lives. World renown physicist Michio Kaku (2014) states, "all the lobes of the brain are devoted to processing signals from our senses, except for one: the frontal lobe, located behind the forehead. The prefrontal cortex, the foremost part of the frontal lobe, is where most rational thought is processed" (p.17).

If students were to write down their emotions, in an essay designed to stimulate "crucial" (critical) thinking, the frontal lobe might be useful to capture the meaning behind the words in the essay and the specific connections to both the essence of the videos and the relevance to the student's understanding of human diversity under uncomfortable circumstances between the public and law enforcement. Hammerness and Moore (2012) state, "functional brain imaging studies have shown when subjects use cognitive strategies to try and reduce negative emotions, an increase of activity can be observed in the cortical, thinking brain, such as the pre-frontal cortex" (p.53) Psychologist Susan David of the Harvard Medical School suggests negative emotions can be clues to our deepest values (Newman, 2017). The Parietal lobe navigates the human areas of touch, taste, and body awareness, as well as coordination of attention.

Students could leverage this region of the brain by interacting with other students in other race or other ethnicity situations during social events that require the tasting of cultural foods, and the touching of hands with others who are not coming from their peer situation or personal culture. Again, the crucial thinking process is fundamental to this experience, so that students can dialog about the cultural differences relative to body awareness, taste, and human touch. In Pittsburgh, Pennsylvania there is an innovative restaurant called ***Conflict Kitchen*** (**Figure N**) that "serves cuisine from countries with which the United States is in conflict. Each Conflict Kitchen iteration is augmented by events, performances, publications, and discussions that seek to expand the engagement the public has with the culture, politics, and issues at stake within the focus region". The restaurant rotates identities in relation to current geopolitical events".

This type of human experience unlocks many unrealized empowerments from several cerebral lobes of the brain in the mind – ranging from speech and smell, to taste and touch, to language and vision. With regards to human diversity, we believe so much of the human potential remains unlocked from full capacity, locked into lower level taxonomical thinking, and unrealized of complete fulfilled manifestation for modern day thought leadership.

Figure N: Conflict Kitchen

(http://conflictkitchen.org/about/)

The Temporal lobe generates the genesis for hearing, memory, and the recognition of faces.

As suggested in ***The Brain: The Ultimate Guide*** (Harris Publications, 2015), the average person can remember as many as ten thousand faces. In addition to those areas listed above, other revelations from *The Brain* that are useful to consider here that relate to human diversity include (**Figure O**):

Figure O: Some Brain Capacities and Capabilities

- *New experiences help shape brain circuits.*
- *The five senses illuminate the world, and the brain is where the information from the environment is interpreted.*
- *The brain devotes more real estate to the processing of visual information, than all other senses combined.*

- *What we see as human beings depends on our own experiences, expectations, and ways of thinking.*
- *Learning and memory are our most precious gifts, without them, nothing else can happen.*
- *Consciousness is a matter of being awake and aware of ourselves and our surroundings.*
- *Intelligence and creativity are linked to how fast our brains work and our own unique neural connections.*
- *There are many brain regions involved in perceptions. It works in an interconnected web of neurons.*
- *We are born with all our neurons and we do not make any more except in the hippocampus, where new information is first processed.*

Perhaps an exploratory experience for students to consider is to list all the faces that can be remembered and determine which faces represent their peer social circumstances and which represent other human faces in diversity from which they have little to no human contact. This type of self-inventory should be useful for helping students identify the extent to which they can remember important faces that are disorienting to them, yet necessary for them to remember as they work with different people in the workplace and throughout communities in which they live, learn, and lead. Given that the brain is changing every minute of the day, from the time of birth to the end of life, adjusting the perceptions that come from the parietal lobe could be most rewarding in this regard and provide a new sense of renewal. We encourage readers to listen (Temporal lobe) to the TED Radio broadcast in 2014 entitled, ***Playing with Perception.***

http: // www.npr.org / programs / ted – radio – hour/358360814/playing -with-perceptions

The Occipital lobe provides the impetus for sight. Butler-Bowden (2015) citing Malcolm Gladwell summarized that "assessments we make in the blink of an eye can be as good as those we make after much deliberation" (p.124). Human beings quite often assess human conditions and circumstances based on what is visualized. The example given for the Frontal lobe is a good example for integrating both regions of the brain to understand human diversity. Nin (2016) suggests that "we do not see things as they are, we see things how we are" (p.15). That said, we would argue the visual metaphysics of what humans see can be clarified more deeply and understood more clearly by challenging the mind in brain to elevate from a taxonomy of lower order crucial thinking to higher order crucial thinking.

We have seen differences in eastern and western cultures, in which western cultures pay more attention to the foreground of a drawing or picture, and eastern cultures focus on the background. In a crucial thinking exercise, students from varying cultural backgrounds (stations, stages, spaces) would probably see different elements of a video or picture with varying perceptions about the human behavior of the victim as well as those in law enforcement. These different perspectives, or perceptions, are bridged from cognitive capacity and crucial thinking.

Questions that may be useful for generating conversations from crucial thinking are offered in ***The Engrossed Entrepreneurial Campus: What Our Academy and Economy Needs Now*** (Stevenson, 2006), which will be discussed later in this essay. Along with these questions, a created mindful taxonomy could build the impetus for moving from lower order thinking to higher order thinking; and from the precepts of human division to the perils of human diversity. The Cerebellum controls not only fine motor skills, muscle navigation, but also human balance and coordination.

Note: The cerebellum is also responsible for automatic, Pavlovian-conditioned or classically conditioned learning and memory. Is it worth it to add this information, since the way our prejudice and discrimination works is at an automatic/implicit level, and would it be good to mention that in a basic way somewhere in the text? We talk about lower vs higher order cognitive processes and crucial thinking, it might be good at the beginning of that topic to mention that a lot of these behaviors we are trying to change or "unlearn" are so ingrained because they are automatic processes, based on our automatic perceptions. And when you talked about emotions, we could also point out that an automatic perception is only strengthened and exacerbated when it is combined with an emotional stimulus. The more emotional a person gets in this state, the more automatic their thoughts and behavior become, and the less likely they are to be able to check their behaviors and thoughts.

Based on the crucial-taxonomical thinking process, it would be interesting to understand student perceptions of body behaviors of all of those involved in the Minneapolis video or other police visual information that would be available concerning the Cambridge video. So far, by bridging cognitive capacity to crucial thinking, we have attempted to build a relationship between neural science and neural social elements that are grounded from the Cerebellum and the Frontal, Parietal, Temporal, and Occipital lobes. The Limbic lobe controls human emotion that range from happiness to sadness and love. This cognitive capacity is probably the most paramount for embracing, accepting, appreciating, and internalizing human diversity on a personal level. The emotions that are ignited from human conflict, yet are needed to understand human diversity, should be a constant part of dialog in classroom or online discussions relative to gender, race, age, culture, ethnicity, and sexual orientation (GRACE) --- in addition to diversity regarding geography, religion, anatomy, class, education, and stratification (GRACE). Indeed, the results of the recent elections in the U.S. revealed disputing perspectives and differing perceptions of GRACE in two very different, yet integrated, mind dimensions.

Caveat #11: "Words Matter" - Michelle Obama (2016)

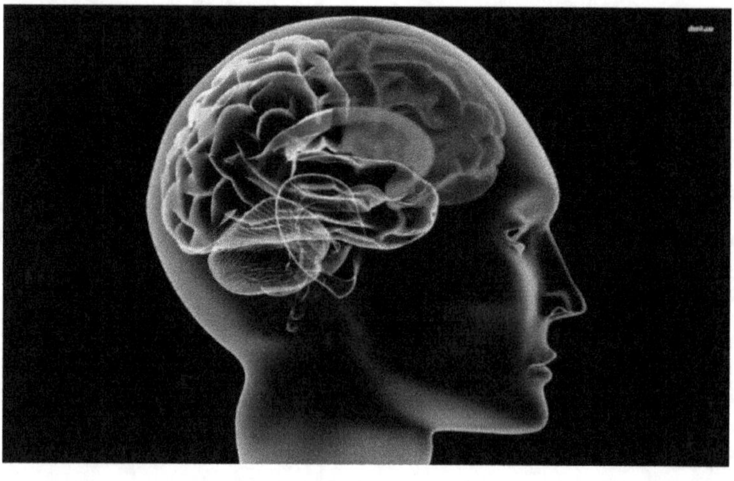

Caveat #12: "Words Can Change Your Brain" - Newberg and Waldman (2013)

Proviso #9

After completion of academic studies or a major class, students will have the ability to identify all regional lobes of the brain and explain their respective potential-possible influences on the brain's navigation of behavior concerning situations, challenges, or circumstances concerning human diversity or human division.

VI.
Crucial Thought
Leadership, Learning and Logic

We have outlined the different regions of the brain that contribute to neural science and neural social relationship building from the capacities of speech, smell, hearing, facial recognition, coordination, vision, motor control, taste, touch, and problem solving.

Other areas that are fundamental to "crucial" (vs. traditional critical) thinking include language and reading, and the extent to which they facilitate the crucial thinking process, from what we visualize and experience through, with and from human interactions. Not surprisingly, humans often assess human conditions from everyday life based on unvetted, unverified, invalid, inappropriate, incomplete, unsubstantiated and inaccurate information. Verifying information, authenticating sources, and validating data related to conflicting situations surrounding human diversity is very crucial to the ***thinking-through-thoroughly-throughout-thought (*****Figure P*****)*** process (Stevenson, Wilson, et al, 2015).

Admittedly, we must also prepare the mind and our behavior when – after verified authentication and evidenced validation – a phenomenon does result in, manifests by and demonstrates from the revelations of an "ism". President Barack Obama recently observed in the "***The Making of a Black President"***, directed and produced by Jackie Lay and Raymond

Schillinger for Atlantic.com/video, that the suspension between the races in part is constructed and created on a constant and daily basis from how people interact and what people see or read without facts and evidence of reality, which taps into the deepest anxieties of people.

We found that when circumstances surrounding certain social events are deeply vetted and broadly verified, certain revelations are revealed that help complete the thought process more fully and on a balanced level. As Pinker (2009) observed, "If only our networks could use a proper learning rule and take in enough data, they would transcend false stereotypes and correctly register the facts of human equality" (p. 313). For instance, if students with a faculty view any of the incidents in Chicago, Charleston, or San Bernardino with complete "climbing" analysis of all variables included, it may be that different perceptions could be developed from framing the following possible taxonomically-related questions from Stevenson's (2006) *The Engrossed Entrepreneurial Campus*:

Figure P: Thinking Things Through Thoroughly Throughout

- *Examine cause, effect, and remedy relationships*
- *Differentiate between fact, opinion, conjecture, and fiction*
- *Determining accuracy and completeness of information*
- *Determine information, originality, or author bias*
- *Contrast, blend, and compare divergent points of view*
- *Recognize logical fallacies and faulty reasoning*
- *Define measurable strategies, objectives, and indicators*
- *Create alternative frameworks for "stretch" thinking*
- *Apply force field analysis for balance and counterbalance*
- *Explore alternatives for resolving conflict and solving problems*
- *Integrating, surmising, and synthesizing information – accurately*

We should note that these above analytical tenets for query and catechism may not necessarily change behavior from mindful exploration; however, they may be useful for the type of mindful activities that were posed earlier with class brainstorming groups assigned by lobe to develop a taxonomy for "thinking things through thoroughly throughout". Resultantly, it may be that these results from the inquiry could lead to informative pretext for understanding behavior before human vulnerabilities occur.

Proviso #10

After completion of studies in their major, students will have the ability to create a human diversity situation, condition, or circumstance that requires cause and effect; fact and opinion; accuracy and incompleteness; and logic and irrational reasoning.

Again, leveraging the metaphor behind *BEFOREWARDS*, what lessons could be learned from viewing unsettling, disconcerting, and disturbing videos concerning diversity – especially considering the widespread and accelerating visual use (Occipital lobe) videos and other digital devices among today's highly impressionable and easily influenced children? How can we train and empower our students and faculty at The Chicago School and other universities with the skills, competencies, attitudes, and dispositions to help communities like Chicago, Illinois, or Charleston, South Carolina, in pro-active, preventative, and prognostic strategies from new upward taxonomical crucial thinking? What could be discerned to differentiate between fact and fiction during these troubling times in Chicago? What could have been the causes and effects from the unsettling situation in Roseburg, Oregon? How can information provided from social media be recognized for possible rhetorical bias or completeness of information reported about the incident? How can force-field analysis of the incidents in San Bernardino, California or Dallas, Texas be examined for contributing factors?

Immordino-Yang (2016) crystalizes many of our points in the book in the following excerpt from her book concerning human emotions, cognitive learning and the capacities of the human brain. She observes:

> *"Think back to the atrocities committed on 9/11. How do we know these actions were wrong? And why do most Americans have such a difficult time understanding how the terrorists could carry out these plans? To decide these things, we automatically, albeit many times non-conscientiously, imagine how the passengers on those planes must have felt, emphatically experiencing both what they were about and their emotions around these thoughts by imagining ourselves in the that fateful plane. For many, just thinking of the images of planes hitting buildings induces a fearful mind-set with all its physiological manifestations, such as a racing heart and anxious thoughts. Similarly, we have difficulty empathizing with the terrorists who brought down the planes, because the values, morals, and emotions that motivated these men are so different from our own" (p.182)*

So, we go back from whence we came. Might we need exhaustive force field analyses examined between external (society) and internal (mind) variables, pressure points, intersections, and confluences? Do we need new valiant, audacious, and intrepid theories constructed amid this apparent point that is increasingly becoming a public health labyrinth? Poteat and Spanierman (2012) found that racial colorblindness is important to address as part of anti-racism education" (p.758). Can racism, sexism, bigotry, misogyny, or homophobia be unlearned? Can human diversity be learned? Could visual images of human anger, anguish or agony manifest in ways that repulse negative behavior or attitude and cultivate positive behavior or attitude toward human diversity? Could the precepts offered in "*Morning Mind: Use Your Brain to Master Your Day and Supercharge Your Life*" be leveraged in preparation for a full day of diversity challenges: Can neurons within the brain be stimulated to create new paradigms, modelling, patterns or actions? Ascending from the metaphor behind *BEFOREWARDS*, what lessons could be learned from these unsettling, alarming and disturbing events?

Obviously, methodologies in qualitative research and quantitative research can provide some utility for addressing some of the issues that manifest from these events through the lenses of a researcher. However, as related to the metaphor behind *BEFOREWARDS*, colleges and universities are likely to make a difference in our broadly broken world by applying these above crucial thinking concepts to situations surrounding human diversity, and by encouraging students to leverage the different regions of the brain to actualize neural social understanding and grasp some of the untapped potential of neural science through the lenses of human psychology. Other areas that should be examined to support our book include social neural science, which is the interdisciplinary understanding of biological systems and how they interact with social, psychological or behavioral processes.

Defining logic as the result of assessment from reasoning, argumentation, probing or rationalization, we see the subliminal significance of the word "**logical**' in both words psycho**logical** and physio**logical**. This is also referenced by Stevenson (2006) as a tenet above for r*ecognizing logical fallacies and faulty reasoning.* Emotional intelligence is another area that should be examined, which identifies the capacity to be aware of, control, or express human emotion and personal feeling. Emotional intelligence factors are fundamental to mindfulness concerning human diversity. Among the compelling realities of contemporary life is the impulse, the anxiety, and the emotion associated with race, racism and race relations. We believe this could be managed through the acceptance, embodiment and embracing of understanding emotional intelligence.

There have been many definitions framed for this human phenomenon since the initial model created by Daniel Goleman in the 1990s, ranging from comprehending and managing emotions on one hand, to navigating thought from perceived emotions on the other hand. However, we recommend the "Four Branch Model of Emotional Intelligence" by Mayer and Salovey (1999, 2000) highlighted below, which reinforces our advocacy for cognitive climbing and cerebral levitation:

- *Accurately perceive emotions in oneself and others*
- *Use emotions to facilitate thinking*
- *Understand emotional meanings, and*
- *Manage emotions*

These four areas for emotion management are most needed and best manifested in the initial analysis of any human diversity challenge. Through the lens from the brain's regional lobes, humans can actively engage in individual or group work that provides the opportunities for mindful self-reflection and validation of perception.

We suggest that the facilitation of mindful thinking should be done through exercises we have described so that humans can apply some or all the critical thinking patterns and principles from the head, to the heart, to the hand. In a classroom setting, students should analyze both perceptions and meanings by bringing their regional lobe back with them to the group settings for group process, feedback, dynamics, reflection, and ultimately transformation. All opinions should be considered important to the individual and group process and the recognition of human imperfection must be accepted. The manifestation of this group work is a genuine learning community of practice. The result of this group work should engage students to think before they talk; analyze before they act; research before they respond; and assemble information and data before they assess the world within from self and around them through others. Emotion should facilitate positive thinking for open-mindedness and mitigate against narrow-mindedness.

When human conflict, related or not related to race, does occur on the college campus in the group, in the classroom, in the dorm, on the field, on the court, or in the quad, all stakeholders should listen to each other; seek to understand the problem; remain calm; be firm (especially about truth); identify needs; apologize when necessary; find real solutions; and explain how decisions will meet a greater resolve (*Change Agents*, pg. 150). Harmful, disheartening and hurtful information that feeds unhealthy thought and fuels inappropriate actions will require students to responsibly study the information and data through the interdependent occurrences, rubrics, questions, and fundamentals in the group work. Our rubric in Figure P can be helpful here.

Students also need "crucial thinking" acumen to caress, comprehend and commit to real human diversity versus human division. This must be re-stated and cannot be combined. Students, as well as all humans, must manage their emotional intelligence from the intellectual acumen and epistemological awareness they develop from crucial thinking, cognitive climbing and cerebral levitation in "other" self, other group, other race, other gender, or other culture situations, settings and spaces. Social psychology is yet another area that would be useful to learn more about as it blends psychology with social interaction from empirical scientific evidence relative to human thoughts, feelings, and other behaviors influenced by human interaction with others. Hook and Howarth (2005) in the ***London School of Economics and Political Science*** recognize that "a variety of possible future directions for a critical psychology of racism/antiracism may assist us in avoiding the trappings of conceptual/methodological homogeneity and disciplinary insularity" (p. 506).

Circling back, the purpose of this book was to frame a conceptual paradigm that bridges the cognitive relationships between the capacity of the human mind and the processes of crucial thinking to better understand diversity and meet some of the challenges that diversity has historically presented in the past and continues to present in contemporary times. Perhaps no other time in human history has human diversity ignited more impact than the last few years in modern higher education. College and university campuses throughout all regions of the United States have been experiencing institutional diversity challenges against individual diversity dimensions.

Religious, spiritual and faith-based diversity has met unprecedented intersections during discourse in higher learning, while there is also the emergence of white pride advocacy. An example of this are the posters from the West Coast Davis campus of the University of California (**Figure Q**). Other similar presentations have been on other college or university campuses. This issue certainly provides students and faculty with a timely opportunity for hierarchal thinking and taxonomical lifting in the context of freedom of speech or expression.

More recently, a story has emerged on the East Coast at "American" University, where the FBI are assisting the University with investigating "bananas found hanging from black nooses"(https://www.nytimes.com/2017/05/03/us/bananas-hang-from-black-nooses-and-a-campus-erupts-in-protest.html?partner=msft_msn&_r=0). Not far from the Washington, D.C. area – just days later -- the same disturbing activity occurred on the College Park campus of the University of Maryland. (http://www.chronicle.com/blogs/ticker/noose-found-on-u-of-maryland-at - college - parks campus / 118193?cid = pm&utm_source = pm&utm_medium=en&elqTrackId=45ad781c5cad4008a741ae49e933ea34&elq=d02ae5b15e544ef987d8035f25c5ae36&elqaid=13789&elqat=1&elqCampaignId=5744)

Perhaps the most horrific, shocking, and heartbreaking fatal campus incident occurred on the campus of Bowie State University, an historically Black (HBCU) institution, also part of the University of Maryland system. The tragic details of this hate crime, that brought national attention to higher education, are sadly highlighted below:

http://www.fox5dc.com/news/local-news/256014720-story

http://ktla.com/2017/05/22/fatal-stabbing-of-black-student-at-university-of-maryland-investigated-as-possible-hate-crime/

Figure Q: White Pride Posters at University of California at Davis (UCD)

(Above from: http://thetab.com/us/uc-davis/2016/11/15/white-pride-posters-appear-at-uc-davis-3084)

Most recently, as of the publication of this book, Martha Pollack, President of Cornell University, metaphorically touching on matters relative to both dismantling democracy and border divisiveness for CNN (2019) in *"America Is Shutting Its Doors to Some of the World's Best Young"* that

> *"Cornell was founded on a principle both simple and revolutionary…an institution where any person can find instruction in any study. Not every person – an impossibility on any campus bound by finite resources – but any person, no matter their race, gender, religion, or nationality. That idea, articulated so clearly over a century and a half ago, mirrors in its ambition the early philosophy of our nation. When the door is open to all, we all thrive. As the national debate over immigration swirls on*

we are at risk of losing sight of that foundational ideal - a trend that endangers our ability as a nation to innovate and compete" (cnn.com).

We believe this three-pound cerebral resource (**Figure R**), gifted to humankind as the brain, is the first place to leverage when one is trying to understand human diversity from cognitive clarity, crucial thought, and concise resolution. How can undergraduates expand this cultural cognition A book that we highly recommend as complementary and companion reading for this book is ***Cross-Cultural Psychology: Critical Thinking and Contemporary Applications*** (2016) by Eric B. Shiraev and David Levy. The human brain equips us to face diversity and the thought processes from the brain empowers the student to discern all variables for finding truth.

We commend the recent efforts by the undergraduate student government of the University of Mississippi to move the confederate statues on campus to an off-campus cemetery location to promote the institution's mission of diversity and inclusiveness. This is a remarkable revelation in higher education.

Our book was not only offered to our professorial colleagues who, like others in our educational system, teach students to be purposeful agents of change in global society but to other professors in the growing global academy who are also charged with the same instructional empowerment to face, confront, and address the human diversity conditions. In short, we ask "What can empower students to think about these most troubling tragedies in a manner that will empower others including those in communities at risk for this kind of violence *before* these troubling, unsettling and disruptive occurrences expand throughout the U.S. and beyond?" Defining authentic "brainstorming" as a work group mechanism for generating new, bold, creative ideas by building on each other's brain print (Makin, 2016) and lexicon (Eichstaedt, 2016) without unconstructive criticism and -- through problem-solving or conflict resolution strategies – may serve to identify untapped potential, unlocked possibilities and unrealized opportunities. Idea mapping could be useful in this regard.

Academically supplemented with peer reviewed sources, another good group resource would be National Geographic's ***Your Brain, A User's Guide, 100 Things You Never Knew*** (2016). This publication was very helpful for a provostial presentation with some group work activities on the Irvine campus of the Chicago School in 2015. Using the above brain graphic as a visual source, and the user guide as a resource, students can explore the possibilities of human diversity relative to the "learning" brain (cells, neurons, memory, language, disorders, intelligence), the "perceptive" brain (eyes, color perception, hearing, listening, smell, tastes, touch, motion) , the "unconscious" brain (illusion, awareness, cycles, sleep, dreaming), the "emotional" brain (mapping, pain, depression, decision-making), and the "aging" brain (memory, learning, coping, dementia).

For instance, could early reading and writing about cognitive climbing with human diversity in one's life mitigate against dementia in later life? Oaklander (2017) recently reported in ***100 New Scientific Discoveries*** that "engaging intellectually with the world across a lifetime through activities like writing letters and reading has been linked in brain autopsies to better cognitive health in old age. Given the myriad and frequency of cognitive climbing that human beings have at their personal and social exposure every day, could there be a link between (a) healthy cognitive exercises for diagnosis of diversity challenges and (b) proactive positioning for healthy mitigation against dementia or other mental disorders?

VII.
Neuroscience,
Neuro-Diversity and Neuro Disorders

One approach is to examine how neuroscience and training diversity can work together in graduate psychology programs. The practice and training of cognitive neuropsychology and neuroscience should respect individual cultural, ethnic, socio-economic, sexual preference and other differences because it acknowledges that individuals learn in their own style in their own cultural and ethnic contexts. Any effort to assess disorder in neuropsychological functioning should take the individual in their cultural and ethnic contexts and affirm individual differences as potential strengths. The professional psychologist in training acknowledges these differences and respects them in assessment and/or treatment of neuropsychiatric disorders, or whatever realm with which the professional psychologist works.

A significant problem is that our diagnostic systems and neuropsychological approaches are very much based on "deficit" or lesion models, i.e., what is the patient missing, or how does the patient deviate from dominant cultural norms, to be considered healthy or normal. Mezzich and colleagues (2010) describe a move away from the current biomedical model of mental disorders in the DSMs to a more person-centered medicine...respect for the patient's autonomy, values, and dignity represents a fundamental recognition of his or her personhood, and an ethical imperative. Slowly these concepts are finding their way into evidence."

> *"By checking off symptoms, whether the patient's responses fulfill diagnostic criteria, we stop asking the patient what she or he experiences. We take interest in the client's responses to the extent that they fulfill our predefined operationalized diagnostic criteria. ... the proposed paradigm shift (i.e., from the biomedical model to a more person-centered medicine) ...provides a more holistic, narrative, strength based (empowering), contextual, and culturally sensitive approach."* (Mishara and Schwartz, 2013).

It follows that the education of today's professional psychology student should include not just neuro-disorders but an emphasis on neuro-diversity that empowers individuals in their various contexts. Just as we are all individuals with distinct fingerprints and personality traits, our brains and bodies may respond differently to treatments and medications. It is hoped that training which combines diversity and neuroscience will encourage today's students of professional psychology to engage in social justice issues as they concern the recent troubling tragedies in a compassionate effort to curtail future ones. One of the authors for this book wrote the following poem about social justice to capture the "global gusts and worldly winds" between the inner and exterior walls of the human brain:

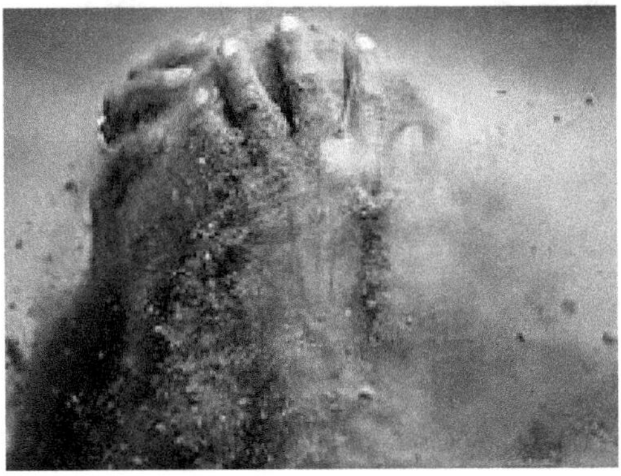

Social Justice is Righteous Reckoning of Balance Between Either Or
Socially Between Me and You
Justice Between Thee and Those Due
Righteousness Between Us and Them
Reckoning Between Adjust and Amend
Balance Between Free and True
Between Global Gust and Worldly Wind
Either by Jubilee from Beginning New
or Dust Ascending from Social Tore
Social Justice is Righteous Reckoning of Balance Between Either Or

(The author uses two definitions from bing.com for the term "dust". As a noun, fine, dry powder consisting of tiny particles of earth or waste matter lying on the ground or on surfaces or carried in the air. As a verb, "beat up or kill someone, "the officers dusted him up a little bit") (https://www.bing.com/search?q=definition+of+dust&FORM=EDGENA)

VIII.
Questions, Challenges and Culmination

We would like to culminate our book with a fitting capstone quote by Gardner (2007), given its most timely context and appropriateness to today's and tomorrow's gauntlets, challenges, and provocations. He most eloquently writes:

> *"Clearly, we can no longer simply draw a curtain or build a wall that isolates from one another indefinitely. We homo sapiens must somehow learn how to inhabit neighboring places – and the same planet – without hating one another , without lusting to injure or kill one another, without acting on xenophobic inclinations even if our own group might emerge triumphant ... Rather than ignoring differences, being inflamed by them, or seeking to annihilate them through love or hate, I call on human beings to accept the differences, learn to live with them, and value who those who belong to other cohorts" (p. 107)*

Pinker (2009) adds, "the question is what to make of any group differences we do stumble upon and here we must be prepared to make a moral judgement. Discrimination against individuals, based on their race, sex, or ethnicity is wrong" (p. 50). Although many laws, statutes, policies, rules, practices, ordinance, decrees, formula and movements have contributed to the progress, successes, and advancement of human diversity over past many decades, recent societal revelations suggest some shortcomings and a need for deeper examination of counter-instance. We believe it is now time to understand the dynamics of human diversity, as well as the drivers of human division, from the momentum, impetus, and genesis where the three-pound (**Figure R**) phenomenon should have been anchored from origin: ***the brain and the human mind. – the three-pound gorilla in the room***.

We need undergraduates to explore new valiant, audacious, and intrepid theories constructed amid our apparent cultural labyrinth. As Neurologist Majid Fotuhi points out about the brain, "it's not just a mysterious box sitting up there, disconnected … it's tightly, tightly connected to the rest of your body, and you can take care of it the same way you can take care of your teeth". (Oaklander, 2017). How can early coded habits and be manifested in this human journey?

"There can be little doubt, the human brain is truly an incredible body organ that requires maximum care to keep vital body processes running".

(From: http: // www.epyk.com /37 / 10 – interesting – facts – about - the-human-brain/3/)

We are asking colleagues to provide voices in our book to ignite transdisciplinary interests and expertise across the arts, sciences, and the professions. It is hoped that our "neuro novo" (*novo* from Latin for new, compound *de novo* meaning anew)book will also begin transdisciplinary dialogue, discourse and discussion about new psychology for children, new cognition for adults, lifelong mindfulness, renewed neuroscience that focuses on human diversity, and new revolutionary theory and research about the mysterious brain.

Figure R: The Three Pound Brain

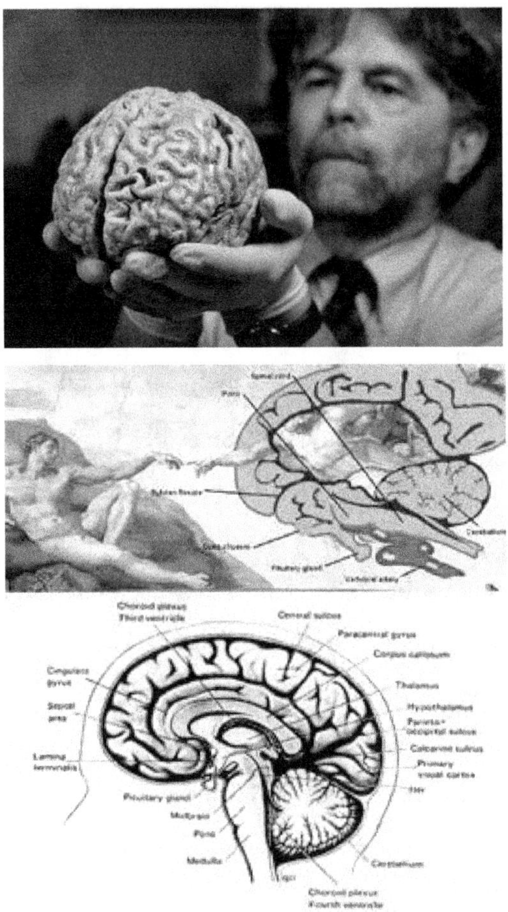

We hope we have made our case for considering human diversity in an old new paradigm – one that may be uncomfortable from looking inward but fundamental to supporting protocols in place to truly make a difference in global diversity and human inclusion. Our "neuro novo" book aims to start dialogue, discourse and discussion about psychology, cognition, mindfulness and brain theory. For students, faculty and other stakeholders we proposed fundamental questions and other probing questions to think about for purposes of intellectual discourse, not to necessarily seek empirical evidence for now – until appropriate research questions are framed with conceptual frameworks to position inquiry for empirically based research on evidence.

We hope that our ***neuro diversity*** book will begin transdisciplinary dialogue, discourse and discussion about psychology, cognition, mindfulness, neuroscience, and brain theory to unlock cerebral empowerment, under-realized cognitive capacity and untapped inner creativity.

Henrich (2011) recognized over a decade ago that "cultural evolution was likely a dominant force driving our species' genetic evolution over the last few hundred thousand years …understanding and theorizing how cultural processes have shaped human evolution provides a framework that unifies and underpins research programs across the social, biological, and historical sciences". We challenge our journal readers to "crucially" consider this transdisciplinary context for exploring phenomenon between brain diversity and behavioral development for the greatest of global human good everywhere, all the time, for everyone, all over the world – perhaps now more than ever when our troubled country is widening division.

Finally, ***National Geographic*** in *"Your Brain: A Users Guide of 100 Things You Never Knew"* (2018) recently suggested that "the human brain and its consciousness contain many mysteries. In recent centuries, scientists have used an increasingly sophisticated variety of tools to find out what happens where-though much is left to learn" (p. 17). The authors of this book hope this reading journey has provided the tools, methods, strategies, and mechanisms to explore the complexities of human diversity as well as human division in this present era of emerging human phenomena.

Caveat #13: "To make progress in our understanding of how cultures shape brains and brains shape culture, we need to know what psychological and behavioral tendencies are associated with these social categories and how these tendencies are linked to brain function."

– Stanford University Professor Hazel Markus (Lende, 2010)

Figure S: Michelangelo's Painting of the Brain and Creation of Adam

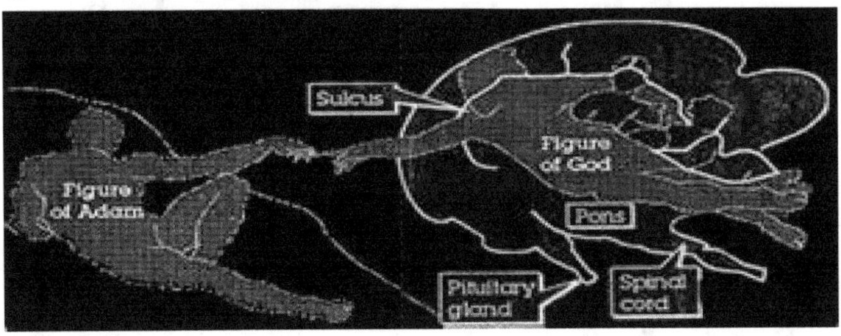

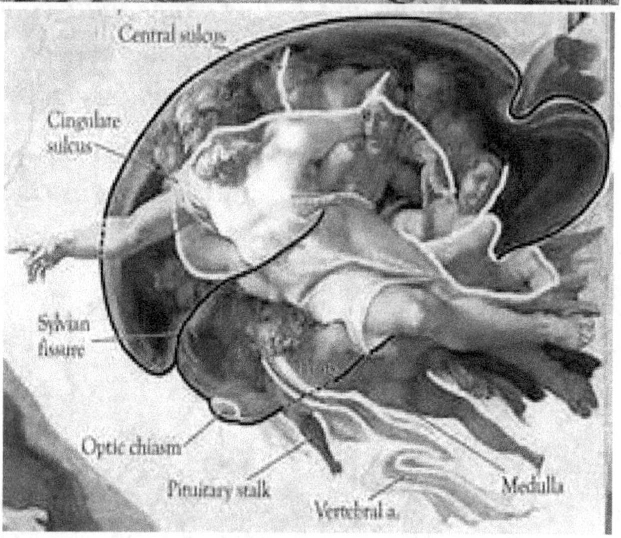

See work of NEUROSURGEONS RAFAEL Tamargo and Ian Suk of Johns Hopkins univeresity, "concealed Neuroanatomy in Michelangelo's sepertaion of light from darkness" in the <u>Journal American medical Association</u> (may 2010, volume 66 issue 5, pp 851-861

(http://www.italianrenaissance.org/michelangelo-creation-of-adam/)

About the authors:

Joseph Martin Stevenson was the first appointed Provost for the Chicago School of Professional Psychology. He now teaches an online class on ethics, social justice and creative leadership for the University of Virgin Island (U.S.) and Union Institute University. He is also a Scholar-In-Residence for Office of the President at Miles College in Birmingham, Alabama. Psychology Professor Jay M. Finkelman, is Chair of the Industrial-Organizational Business Psychology Department for the Southern California campuses of The Chicago School of Professional Psychology, where Bryant Horowitz is Adjunct Faculty. Melissa Druckrey is the Dean of Libraries at Jackson State University, and Karen Wilson Stevenson is a senior higher education administrator and Certified Fund-Raising Executive who is completing a PhD in higher education leadership at Jackson State University.

*The above graphical images highlight Michelangelo's painting of the brain and creation of Adam -- representing to some -- the beginning of humankind. We note again, consciously looking inward focuses on the "**me**" and "**i**" in **Ame**ric**a**.*

References

(Other references or citations are also subsumed in the Book)

7 Billion human brains. (2019). Retrieved from https://sapienlabs.co

Aamodt, S. and Wang, S. (2009). *Welcome to your brain*. New York, NY: MJF Book.

Allee, V. (2003). The future of knowledge: Increasing prosperity through value networks. Oxford: Butterworth-Heinemann.

Bass, L. (2012). Overcoming cultural collision in educational leadership. In C. Gerstl-Pepin & J. A. Aiken (Eds.), *Social justice leadership for a global world*. IAP, Inc: Charlotte. www.infoagepub.com

Bianchi, A. (2004). Primary influence on diversity [Web log post]. Retrieved from www.thehumanequation.com/en/news_rss/articles/2004/Primary_Influences_on_Diversity.aspx

Brett Szymik. (2011). A Nervous Journey. ASU - *Ask A Biologist*. Retrieved December 17, 2015 from http://askabiologist.asu.edu/what-your-brain-doing

Brockman, M (2011). *Future Science: Essays from the Cutting Edge*. New York, NY: Vintage/Random House.

Butler-Bowdon, T. (2015). *50 Psychology Classics: Who We Are, How We Think, What We Do*. London: Nicholas Brealey.

Carter, R. & Carter, K. S. (2019). *The morning mind: Use your brain to master your day and supercharge your life*. New York: Harper Collins Leadership Publications.

Daniels, P., & Kashdan, T. B. (2016). Mind*: A scientific guide to who you are, how you got that way, and how to make the most of it.* Washington, D.C.: National Geographic.

David, S. (2017). *Emotional agility: Get unstuck, embrace change, and thrive in work and life.* Great Britain: Penguin Life.

Davidson, C. (2011). *Now you see it: How the brain science of attention will transform the way we live, work, and learn*. New York, NY: Penguin.

Devlin, H. (2017). AI programs exhibit racial and gender biases, research reveals. Retrieved April 13, 2017 from the Guardian https://www.theguardian.com/

technology/2017/apr/13/ai-programs-exhibit-racist-and-sexist-biases-research-reveals

Eagleman, D. (2011). *Incognito: The secret lives of the brain.* New York: First Vintage Books.

Eagleman, D. (Writer). (2015). The brain with David Eagleman [Television series episode]. In The brain with David Eagleman. PBS.

Eichstaedt, J. C. (2016). Status Update: Stressed, Angry, At Risk? *Scientific American Mind,* 27(2), 62-67. doi: 10.1038/scientificamericanmind0316-62

Finn, E. S., Shen, X., Scheinost, D., Rosenberg, M. D., Huang, M. M., Constable, R. T. (2015). Functional connectome fingerprinting: Identifying individuals using patterns of brain connectivity. Nature Neuroscience, 18(11), 1664-1671. doi:10.1038/nn.4135

Ferraro, V. (2015, October 18). In the Heat of the Moment: Take a Journey through Bias Awareness and Kindness. [Web log post]. Retrieved from (www.mindful.com)

Firestien, R. (2017, February 1). The power of incubation. [Web log post]. Retrieved from https://rogerfirestien.com/the-power-of-incubation/

Firestien, R. (2017 March 1). Making the RIGHT Mistakes/Solve the Right Problem. [Web log post]. Retrieved from https://rogerfirestien.com/blog

Frame, J. D. (2013). *Framing decisions: Decision making that accounts for irrationality, people and constraints*. San Francisco, CA: Jossey Bass.

Frey, W. H. (2014). *The diversity explosion: How new racial demographics are remaking america*. [Kindle]. Retrieved from https://www.amazon.com

Gardner, H. (1993). *Frames of the Mind: The theory of multiple intelligences*. New York, NY: Basic Books.

Gardner, H. (2008). Five minds for the future. Boston: Harvard Business School Press.

Hall, M.P. (2005). Bridging Heart and Mind: Community as a Device for Linking Cognitive and Affective Learning. *Journal of cognitive learning*, 1, 8-12.

Hammerness, P. & Moore, M. (2012). *Organize your mind organize your life*. Ontario: Harvard University/Harlequin.

Han, S. (2015). Understanding cultural differences in human behavior: A cultural neuroscience approach. *Current Opinion in Behavioral Sciences*, 3, Pages, 68-72. doi:10.1016/j.cobeha.2015.01.013

Harland, B. (2014). Mintel: What you need to know about diversity in the US video game industry. [Web log post]. Retrieved from http://www.mintel/com/blog/technology-market-news/video-game-trends

Harris, D. (2000). *Change agents: New rules for communicating with employees*. Salt Lake City, UT: Franklin Covey.

Henrich, J. (November 2011). A cultural species: How culture drove human evolution. *Psychological Science Agenda*. Retrieved from https://www.apa.org/science/about/psa/2011/11/human-evolution

Hook, D. & Howarth, C. (2005). Future Directions for a Critical Social Psychology of Racism/Antiracism. *Journal of community and applied social psychology*, 15, 506-512.

Howard, P. J. (2014). The owner's manual for the brain: The ultimate guide to peak mental performance at all ages. New York, NY: William Morrow, an imprint of HarperCollins.

Immordino-Yang, M.H. (2016). *Emotions learning, and the brain: Exploring the educational implications of affective neuroscience*. New York, NY: W.W. Norton & Company.

Lende, D. (2010). Neuroanthropogy: Understanding the Encultured Brain and Body. [Web log post]. Retrieved at http://blogs.plos.org/neuroanthropology/2010/11/26/cultural-neuroscience-%e2%80%93-culture-and-the-brain/

Lewis, K. R. (2014). The next frontier in workplace diversity: Brain differences. Retrieved from http://fortune.com/2014/12/16/brain-differences-autism-workplace-diversity/

Kaku, M (2014). *The future of the mind: The scientific quest to understand, enhance, and empower the mind.* New York: Anchor/ Random House.

Kashdan, T. (2016). Foreword: Exploring the Mind in *Mind: A scientific guide to who you are, how you get that way, and how to make the most of it*. Washington, D.C. National Geographic.

Kuhn, T.S. (1970). *The structure of scientific revolutions* (2nd Ed.). Chicago, IL: University of Chicago.

Lequerica, A. & Krch, D. (2014). Issues pf Cultural Diversity in Acquired Brain Injury (ABI) Rehabilitation. *NeuroRehabilitation* 34(4), 645-653.

Levitin, D. (2015). *The organized mind*. New York, NY: Plume/Penguin.

Linker, M. (2014). *Intellectual empathy: Critical thinking for social justice*. Dearborn, MI: University of Michigan Press.

Makin, S. (2016). The Brain's Whorl. *Scientific American*, 314(1), 22.

Markman, A. and Duke, B. (2016). *Brain briefs: Answers to the most (and least) pressing questions about your mind*. New York, NY: Sterling.

Mays, V., Johnson, D., Coles, C., Gellene, D., & Cochran (2013). Using the science of psychology to target perpetrators of racism and race -based discrimination for intervention efforts: Preventing another Trayvon

Martin tragedy. *Journal of Social Action in Counseling and Psychology, 5*(1), 11-36.

McClure, S. (2011). Our brains know why we do what we do. In M. Brockman (Ed.), *Future Science*. New York, NY: Vantage/Random House.

Meissner, P & Wulf, T. (2016). The effect of cognitive diversity on the illusion of control bias in strategic decisions: An experimental investigation. *European Management Journal*, XXX, 1-10.

Mezzich J., Snaedal J., Van Weel C., & Heath I. (2010). Toward person-centered medicine: From disease to patient to person. *Mount Sanai Journal of Medicine*, 77, 304-306.

Mishara, A.L., & Schwartz, M.A. (2013). What does phenomenology contribute to the debate about DSM-5? In J. Paris & J. Phillips (Eds), *Conceptual and pragmatic issues in DSM-5*. New York, NY: Springer.

National Geographic. (2016). Your Brain, A User's Guide, 100 Things You Never Knew. Washington, D.C.

Newberg, A. & Waldman, M.R. (2013). *Words can change your brain*. New York, NY: Penguin.

Newman, K. M. (2017). What to do when you feel stuck in negative emotions. *Mindful: Taking Time for What Matters*. www.mindful.org

Nin, A. (2016). The science of the mind. Mind: A scientific guide to who you are, how you get that way, and how to make the most of it. Washington, DC: National Geographic.

No Health without Mental Health Report (2016). The Chicago School of Professional Psychology. Los Angeles, CA.

Oaklander, M. (2017). The mind: Untangling Alzheimer's. *In 100 new scientific discoveries: Fascinating momentous and mind-expanding breakthroughs*. New York, NY: Time Books.

Parry, M. (2017, January 22). Brains from Which the Alt-Right Sprang. Retrieved from https://www.chronicle.com/article/Brains-from-Which-the/238025

Paul, R. and Elder, L. (1997) Foundation For, Online at website: www.criticalthinking.org)

Peters, A. (2004). The selfish brain: Competition for energy resources. *Neuroscience & Biobehavioral Reviews*. doi:10.1016/s0149-7634(04)00025-9

Pettijohn, T.F., II & Watzer, A.S. (2008). Reducing Racism, Sexism, and Homophobia in College Students by Completing a Psychology of Prejudice Course. *College Student Journal*. 42(2), 459-468.

Pinker, S. (2009). *How the mind works*. Brilliance Audio. London: W.W. Norton and Company.

Pollack, M. (2019). America is shutting its doors to some of the world's best young minds. Retrieved from https://www.cnn.com/2019/03/04/opinions/trump-immigration-international-students-research-universities-pollack/index.html

Positive Psychology Program - Your One-Stop Positive Psychology Resource (2016). Retrieved from https://positivepsychologyprogram.com/founding-fathers/)

Poteat, V. P. & Spanierman L.B. (2012). Modern racism attitudes among white Students: The role of dominance and authoritarianism and the mediating effects of racial color-blindness. *The Journal of Social Psychology*, 152(6), 758-774.

Rosenblum, F. (2017). Power and politics: A threat to the global brain. *Technological Forecasting and Social Change*, 114, 43-47.

Russ, S. (2016). Sparking creativity: How parents and even video games can spur it in kids. THINK: The Magazine of Case Western Reserve University, Fall/Winter 2016, 9.

Seth, A. and Frith, C. (2017). 30-Second brain: The 50 most mind-blowing ideas in neuroscience, each explained in half a minute. New York NY: Metro Books.

Siegel, J. (2017). Mind: A journey to the heart of being human. New York, NY: Norton.

Schmahmann JD. (2004). Disorders of the cerebellum: Ataxia, dysmetria of thought, and the cerebellar cognitive affective syndrome. *The Journal of Neuropsychiatry and Clinical Neurosciences*, 16(3), 367-78.

Smith, K., & Rock, D. (2018). Approaching diversity with the brain in mind. Retrieved from https://strategy-business.com/article/approaching-diversity-with-the-brain-in-mind

Sternberg, E. J. (2016). *Neurologic: The brain's hidden rationale behind our irrational behavior*. New York, NY: Pantheon Books.

Stevenson, J.M. (2006). *The engrossed entrepreneurial campus: What our academy and economy need now*. Palo Alto: CA: Academica Press.

Stevenson, J.M. (2015). Diversity Leadership for America and Beyond. Testimony and Presentation for President Barack Obama's White House Initiatives on Historically Black Colleges and Universities. Spring, 2015. Washington, D.C.

Stevenson, J. M. and Leahy, M.J. (2015). Teaching agents of change for social justice and responsibility; a possible field guide. *The TCS System Retreat at Pacific Oaks College*. Pasadena, CA: Pacific Oaks College.

Stevenson, J.M., Wilson, K.C., McLin, D.B., & Walker, R.E. (2015). *THEORRY: The higher education of research & resource yield = THEORRY*. Palo Alto, CA: Academica Press.

Sundem, G. ((2012). *Brain trust: 93 top scientists reveal lab-tested secret to surfing, dating, dieting, gambling, growing man-eating plants and more*! New York NY: Penguin/Random House.

Szymik, Brett. (2011). A nervous journey [Web log post]. Retrieved December 17, 2015 from http://askabiologist.asu.edu/what-your

Ugur, H., Constantinescu, P.M., & Stevens, M. J. (2015). Self awareness and personal growth: Theory and application of bloom's taxonomy. *Eurasian Journal of Educational Research*, 15(60), 89-110.

U of Mississippi student leaders: Move confederate statue. (2019). Retrieved from https://www.voanews.com/a/u-of-mississippi-student-leaders-move-confederate-statue/4816842.html

U.S. Department of Labor Study. (2010). *The changing workplace: Family education.* Washington DC: U.S. Government Printing Office.

United States. Department of Labor. (2001). *Futurework: Trends and challenges for work in the 21st century.* Washington DC: U.S. Government Printing Office.

University of California - Los Angeles. (2007, July 23). Culture influences brain cells: Brain's mirror neurons swayed by ethnicity and culture. *ScienceDaily*. Retrieved March 7, 2019 from www.sciencedaily.com/releases/2007/07/070718002115.htm

The video game industry has a diversity problem that runs deeper than race and gender. (2015, March). Retrieved from https://www.theguardian.com/technology/2017/mar/15/video-game-industry-diversity-

Caveat #14: Implicit bias or social cognition is the process by which the brain uses "mental associations that are so well-established as to operate without awareness, or without intention, or without control."

https:// implicit.harvard.edu / implicit / demo / background / faqs. html#faq2

Figure T: Images of The Present American Psyche

Caveat #15: ***"Human diversity makes tolerance more than a virtue: it makes it a requirement for survival".***

-Rene Dubos

How can undergraduates take the nerve to build bold, new cultural virtues for humankind's survival with neuro diversity within our dividing nation?

Appendix - A

(Prepared by TCSPP Professor Bryant Horowitz; see also social media on incidents in Sacramento and Baton Rouge)

People of Color (Unarmed) Killed by Police

Freddie Gray- Baltimore, MD (Apr 12, 2015)

Gray was arrested by police in Baltimore for possessing what the police alleged was an illegal switchblade. While being transported in a police van, Gray fell into a coma and was taken to a trauma center. Gray died on April 19, 2015; his death was ascribed to injuries to his spinal cord. On April 21, 2015, pending an investigation of the incident, six Baltimore police officers were suspended with pay. The circumstances of the injuries were initially unclear; eyewitness accounts suggested that the officers involved used unnecessary force against Gray while arresting him—a claim denied by at least one officer involved. Commissioner Anthony W. Batts reported that, contrary to department policy, the officers did not secure him inside the van while transporting him to the police station. The medical investigation found that Gray had sustained the injuries while in transport. The policy had been put into effect six days prior to Gray's arrest, following review of other transport-related injuries sustained during police custody in the city and elsewhere in the country during the preceding years. Freddie Gray was 25 years old.

Aftermath: First and foremost, this has followed a string of black person targeted police misconduct and incited a city-wide riot in the streets of Baltimore, even more violent than the protests and civil disorder in Ferguson, Missouri. The riots in Baltimore caused a state of unrest which resulted in 34 arrests and injuries to 15 police officers, as well as looting and the burning down of local businesses. A state of emergency was declared by the governor of Maryland.

Walter Scott- Charleston, SC (Apr 4, 2015)

In South Carolina, a white police office, Michael Slager, was caught on video chasing down Walter Scott, an African American male. Slager stopped Scott in a parking lot for a broken taillight and asked him to get out of the vehicle. Scott responded by taking off with Slager chasing after him. What was caught on a cell phone video was Slager firing at Scott. The video itself picks up during the chase, after Scott runs off. Slager is seen shooting at Scott eight times as he runs away from the vacant lot. Scott drops to the ground after the last shot and Slager walks over calmly and is shown handcuffing Scott's arms behind his back. Other police officers and later EMS tried to administer CPR, but Scott died at the scene, according to an incident report. The officer claimed that the suspect took his taser from him and that he feared for his life. In fact, in the video you can hear Slager calling it in: "Shots fired. Subject is down. He grabbed my Taser," Slager says in a call to dispatchers. What could also be seen on video was the officer seeming to plant the taser next to Scott, to corroborate with the story. Scott was 50 years old.

Aftermath: Slager was arrested less than an hour after the video was provided to city and police officials. The family of Scott said he probably ran because he owed child support.

The Justice Department and the South Carolina Office of the FBI are also reviewing the incident, which comes on the heels of other police-related deaths involving unarmed black males in the St. Louis suburb of Ferguson, Cleveland and New York's Staten Island.

Michael Brown- Ferguson, MO (Aug 9, 2014)

Shortly before the shooting, Brown stole several packages of cigarillos from a nearby convenience store and shoved the store clerk. Wilson had been notified by police dispatch of the robbery and the suspect's description. He encountered Brown and Dorian Johnson as they were walking down the middle of the street. Although Wilson's initial contact with Brown and Johnson was unrelated to the robbery, Wilson said that he recognized that the two men matched the robbery suspect descriptions. Wilson backed up his cruiser and blocked them. An altercation ensued with Brown and Wilson struggling through the window of the police vehicle until Wilson's gun was fired. Brown and Johnson then fled, with Wilson in pursuit of Brown. Brown stopped and turned to face the officer. The entire interaction eventually resulted in Officer Wilson firing at him several times, all striking him in the front. In the entire altercation, Wilson fired a total of twelve bullets; the last was probably the fatal shot. Brown was unarmed. Brown was moving toward Wilson when the final shots were fired. Witness reports differed as to what Brown was doing with his hands when he was shot, but no credible witness said that he had his hands up in surrender. Wilson reported that Brown "looked like a demon." Michael Brown was 18 years old.

Aftermath: Wilson was not indicted by a grand jury. He resigned from the Ferguson police force. "The family greatly wanted to have the killer of their unarmed son held accountable. The shooting sparked unrest in Ferguson. Protests, both peaceful and violent, along with vandalism and looting, continued for more than a week, resulting in night curfews. The response of area police agencies in dealing with the protests received significant criticism from the media and politicians. There were concerns over insensitivity, tactics and a militarized response.

Missouri Governor Jay Nixon ordered local police organizations to cede much of their authority to the Missouri State Highway Patrol.

Eric Garner- New York, NY (July 17, 2014)

Police alleged they saw Garner selling illegal untaxed cigarettes, but Garner had broken up a fight just prior to his death, which may have drawn Orta's and Officer Daniel Pantaleo's attention to him. After an argument where Garner told them "Get away [garbled] for what? Every time you see me, you want to mess with me. I'm tired of it. It stops today. Why would you...? Everyone standing here will tell you I didn't do nothing. I did not sell nothing. Because every time you see me, you want to harass me. You want to stop me [garbled] selling cigarettes. I'm minding my business, officer, I'm minding my business. Please just leave me alone. I told you the last time, please just leave me alone." Officer Daniel Pantaleo placed Garner in a chokehold. Garner died of neck compression from the chokehold along with "the compression of his chest and prone positioning during physical restraint by police." Garner is heard saying "I can't breathe" multiple times while lying face down on the sidewalk. The chokehold, incidentally, has been outlawed in New York for at least the last 20 years. Eric Garner was 43.

Aftermath: The New York City medical examiner ruled Garner's death a homicide. Pantaleo was not indicted. On August 1, Garner's death was found by the New York City Medical Examiner's Office to be a result of "compression of neck (chokehold), compression of chest and prone positioning during physical restraint by police". Asthma, heart disease, and obesity were cited as contributing factors. The incident was caught on video and clearly you could hear Garner yelling "I can't breathe, I can't breathe", which was used as a slogan when protesters came and showed their dismay for the situation. Al Sharpton organized a protest in Staten Island on the afternoon of July 19 and condemned the police's use of the chokehold on Garner, saying that "there is no justification" for it. On July 29, a protest organized by WalkRunFly Productions and poet Daniel J. Watts was held in Times Square. The protest was in the form of poetry and many Broadway entertainers participated in the event. After the Staten Island grand jury decided not to indict Pantaleo on December 3, people in New York City and San Francisco gathered in protest. On December 5, thousands gathered in protest on the Boston Common in Boston, and then marched around the downtown area, blocking traffic, in addition to staging "die-ins". Protests also occurred in Chicago, Washington, D.C., Baltimore, Minneapolis, and Atlanta.

Tamir Rice- Cleveland, OH (Nov 22, 2014)

A rookie Cleveland police officer responding to a 911 call jumped out of a cruiser and within seconds shot and killed a 12-year-old boy wielding what later turned out to be a BB gun. Officer Tim Loehman shot and killed Rice, just seconds after spotting him at a park. Video footage of this incidence was captured and made public at the request of Tamir's family. The video shows one thing distinctly: the police officers reacted quickly," reads a statement from the family, who also called on the community to remain calm. The video shows a man calling 911 about Rice, claiming he was "pointing it at everybody". But he also said the gun is "probably fake" and "IU don't know if it is real or not". Apparently, this information wasn't mentioned to the officers approaching the scene.

Aftermath: The video's release comes after days of protests in Cleveland, centered on Tamir's death as well as the community response to the grand jury decision in the shooting of unarmed teenager Michael Brown in Ferguson. Rice's family has filed a wrongful death lawsuit against the city of Cleveland. The year before, the U.S. Justice Department opened an investigation into the Cleveland Police over allegations of excessive and unreasonable deadly force. Within hours of the video's release Wednesday, several Cleveland organizations called to demonstrate the shooting, according to the Plain Dealer. About 200 protesters had gathered in a city square the night before and spilled into the street in a mostly peaceful protest, the paper reported. By early Wednesday night, a handful of protesters had come out, but the video's release didn't spark immediate mass demonstrations.

Trayvon Martin - Sanford, FL (Feb 26, 2012)

Fatally shot by George Zimmerman (neighborhood watch) wearing a hoodie and walking to a family member's home after leaving a convenience store. Zimmerman shot Martin, who was unarmed, during an altercation between the two. Trayvon Martin was 17 years old. Aftermath:

Zimmerman was taken into custody, treated for head injuries, and then questioned for five hours. The police chief said that Zimmerman was released because there was no evidence to refute Zimmerman's claim of having acted in self-defense, and that under Florida's Stand Your Ground statute, the police were prohibited by law from making an arrest. The police chief also said that Zimmerman had had a right to defend himself with lethal force.

Aftermath: As news of the case spread, thousands of protesters across the country called for Zimmerman's arrest and a full investigation. Six weeks after the shooting, amid widespread, intense, and in some cases misleading media coverage, Zimmerman was charged with murder by a special prosecutor appointed by Governor Rick Scott. Zimmerman's trial began on June 10, 2013, in Sanford. On July 13, 2013, a jury acquitted him of second-degree murder. On 24 February 2015, the Justice Department announced that "there was not enough evidence for a federal hate crime prosecution." Protests were staged around the U.S. prior to Zimmerman's April 11 indictment on murder charges. Over 2.2 million signatures were collected on a Change.org petition, created by Martin's mother, calling for Zimmerman's arrest. It was the website's largest petition ever. Since Martin was killed while wearing a hoodie, hoodies were used as a sign of protest over the handling of the case. Additionally, some professional athletes, including Carmelo Anthony, Dwyane Wade, LeBron James, and the entire Miami Heat roster, donned hoodies in Martin's honor. Bags of Skittles candy and cans of Arizona Iced Tea were also used as protest symbols as he was reported to be returning from a 7-Eleven with these items when he was shot. Walkouts were staged by students at over a dozen Florida high schools, and thousands of people attended rallies around the country to demand Zimmerman's arrest. Members of the Occupy movement marched in solidarity during the "Million Hoodie March".

Oscar Grant III - Oakland, CA (Jan 1, 2009)

Oscar Grant III was fatally shot by BART Police officer Johannes Mehserle in Oakland, California, United States, in the early morning hours of New Year's Day 2009. Responding to reports of a fight on a crowded Bay Area Rapid Transit train returning from San Francisco, BART Police officers detained Grant and several other passengers on the platform at the Fruitvale BART Station. Officer Johannes Mehserle and another officer were restraining Grant, who was lying face down and handcuffed. Officer Mehserle stood and, according to his attorney, said: "Get back, I'm gonna Tase him." Then Mehserle drew his pistol and shot Grant once in the back. During his court testimony, Mehserle said that Grant then exclaimed, "You shot me!" Grant was unarmed; he was pronounced dead the next morning at Highland Hospital in Oakland. The events were captured on multiple digital video and cell phone cameras. The footage was disseminated to media outlets and to various websites, where it was watched millions of times. The following days saw both peaceful and violent protests.

Aftermath: On January 30, 2010, Alameda County prosecutors charged Mehserle with murder for the shooting. He resigned his position and pleaded not guilty. The trial began on June 10, 2010. Michael Rains, Mehserle's criminal defense attorney, argued that Mehserle mistakenly shot Grant with his pistol, intending to use his Taser when he saw Grant reaching for his waistband. Pretrial filings argue that his client did not commit first-degree murder and asked a Los Angeles judge to instruct the jury to limit its deliberations to either second-degree murder or acquittal. On July 8, 2010, the jury returned its verdict: Mehserle was found guilty of involuntary manslaughter and not guilty of second-degree murder and voluntary manslaughter. Though initial protests after the ruling were peacefully organized, looting, arson, destruction of property, and small riots broke out after dark. Nearly 80 people were eventually arrested.

Those are the men that made the national news. There are still many others who did not receive the same caliber of media attention. Here are the stories of the other African American men and boys who lost their lives, and were unarmed (from 1999-2015):

Brendan Glenn - Venice, CA (May 5, 2015)

On the night of May 5, 2015, police got a call of a homeless man disturbing the customers near the Venice Boardwalk. He seemed to be intoxicated and got into an altercation with a bouncer at a bar. Police tried to detain him and got into an altercation before one policeman stepped back and fired two shots at Glenn, who was pronounced dead at the hospital. Glenn was 29 years old. He had problems with alcohol but was searching for jobs with the help of a local shelter type business to get back on his feet. **Aftermath:** Autopsy and investigations are still pending.

Rumain Brisbon - Phoenix, AZ (Dec 2, 2014)

A white police officer who was feeling threatened used lethal force on an unarmed black man. The incident left the officer unharmed and Brisbon, dead with two bullet wounds in his torso at a north Phoenix apartment complex. The unarmed father of 4 was shot to death when a police officer apparently mistook his bottle of pills for a gun. Brisbon was 34.

Akai Gurley - Brooklyn, NY (Nov 20, 2014)

Gurley was shot in the stairwell of an East NY housing project building by Officer Peter Liang. Gurley was unarmed. Police Commissioner William Bratton called Gurley a “total innocent”. The cop who stood behind Liang doesn’t know what happened; the girlfriend didn’t know what happened. A quote from the NY times by another officer claims “There is a distinct possibility that Officer Liang doesn’t quite understand what happened”. Gurley was 28 years old. **Aftermath:** District Attorney Ken Thompson is investigating the matter.

Kajieme Powell - St Louis, MO (Aug 19, 2014)

Powell was shot by police who responded to a 911 call accusing him of stealing some energy drinks and pastries. Cops claimed that he approached them holding a knife "in an overhand grip"; video footage of the incident shows that Powell did not come as close to the police as they reported and that his hands were by his side. Police shot him within 15 seconds of arriving at the scene. He was just 25 years old. **Aftermath:** Powell's family has filed a wrongful death suit against the St. Louis police chief and arresting officers.

Ezell Ford - Los Angeles, CA (Aug 12, 2014)

Ford was shot by police who were conducting "an investigative stop." "A struggle ensued," read the LAPD's news release. Ford's family members say he was lying down when shot. Ezell was 25 years old. Aftermath: The LAPD, which hasn't closed the investigation into Ford's death, put an indefinite "investigative hold" on the coroner's autopsy report to prevent witness testimony from being tainted.

Dante Parker - Victorville, CA (Aug 12, 2014)

Police responded to a call about an attempted break-in. The suspect fled on a bicycle. Police found Parker nearby riding his bike. He was unarmed. He resisted arrest and a struggle ensued. Police tasered him and he died. He was 36 years old. **Aftermath:** Pending. The NAACP has called for a federal investigation.

John Crawford III - Beavercreek, OH (Aug 5, 2014)

Crawford was fatally shot while carrying a pellet gun in a Wal-Mart. The gun was unsold merchandise and out of its package. A man named Ronald Ritchie told 911 that he looked like he was pointing it at people, but a month later he admitted that Crawford was not pointing the gun at people. John was 22 years old. According to Ritchie at the time, Crawford was pointing the gun at people and at children walking by and loading bullets into the gun. Ritchie has since recanted, stating "At no point did he shoulder the rifle and point it at somebody". **Aftermath:** No indictment.

Tyree Woodson - Baltimore, MD (Aug 2, 2014)

Police say Woodson's fatal gunshot wound was self-inflicted. That would mean that he smuggled his gun into a police station after police brought him there for having several open warrants. "Things don't seem quite right here," said Baltimore Councilman Carl Stokes. "This person could have a gun, a high caliber gun, that could be used against other officers and then he allegedly kills himself." Tyree was 38 years old. **Aftermath:** Still pending (most people do not know there was a separate incident in Baltimore).

Victor White III - Iberia Parish, LA (Mar 22, 2014)

The coroner says he shot himself while handcuffed in the back of a police cruiser. The autopsy report claims, White's injuries "are possible to be self-inflicted even with the hands handcuffed behind the back." "Short of him being Houdini or David Copperfield, it's not possible," said White's family's attorney. Victor was 22 years old. **Aftermath:** Pending. District Attorney Phil Haney of the 16th Judicial Circuit, who said he will let a federal investigation run its course before deciding.

McKenzie Cochran - Southfield, MI (Jan 28, 2014)

Cochran died of "position compression asphyxia" during struggle with mall security. Cochran told them, "I can't breathe" (Similar to Garner). This incident was also captured via cell phone video. His death ruled an accident by medical examiner. McKenzie was 25 years old. **Aftermath:** No indictments for the security guards. (And no description of the mall security guards found).

Jordan Baker - Houston, TX (Jan 16, 2014)

An off-duty police officer thought Baker fit the description of robbery suspects—both they and he were wearing black hooded sweatshirts. A scuffle and foot chase ensued. Baker, who was unarmed, was fatally shot. Jordan was 26 years old. Aftermath: Officer J. Castro, who killed Baker, was placed on administrative leave pending an investigation. Baker's mother was said to be considering filing a lawsuit.

Andy Lopez - Santa Rosa, CA (Oct 22, 2013)

Lopez was carrying a pellet gun that resembled an AK-47 assault rifle. After officers reportedly told Lopez to drop the gun, he turned toward them, and they shot him. He was 13 years old. Aftermath: No indictment.

Jonathon Ferrell - Bradfield Farms, NC (Sep 14, 2013)

Ferrell crashed his car and knocked on the door of a nearby house. The woman inside called the police. Police said that when Ferrell was apprehended, they shot him. Ten times. He was 24 years old. **Aftermath**: Officer Randall Kerrick has been indicted on a charge of voluntary manslaughter. It took two grand juries to get there.

Carlos Alcis - New York, NY (Aug 15, 2013)

Alcis died of a heart attack after the police mistakenly raided his home in search of a cell phone thief. He was 43 years old. Aftermath: Alcis' family has filed a wrongful death suit against the city and the NYPD for $10 million.

Larry Eugene Jackson, Jr. - Austin, TX (July 26, 2013)

Jackson was fatally shot during a scuffle resulting from a chase that took place when detective Charles Kleinert apprehended Jackson for trying to "defraud" a bank. Larry was 32 years old. **Aftermath**: Kleinert was indicted on a manslaughter charge.

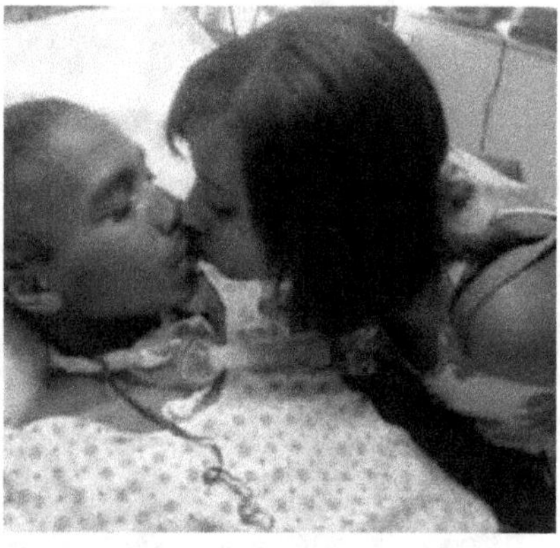

Deion Fludd - New York, NY (May 5, 2013)

Police say that a train clipped Fludd as they chased him after dodging subway fare. According to his mother, Fludd denied this before succumbing to his injuries. He was 17 years old. **Aftermath**: Fludd's mother sued the officers involved, the NYPD, and the MTA.

Kimani Gray - New York, NY (Mar 9, 2013)

Police said Gray pointed a revolver at them as they attempted to question him. Friends and family say Gray had never had a gun, and a witness says he never pointed one at police. The cops shot a total of 11 rounds, striking Gray several times. Kimani Gray was 16 years old. **Aftermath:** No indictments for the cops responsible for shooting Gray.

Johnnie Kamanhi Warren - Dotham, AL (Dec 10, 2012)

A Houston County Sheriff's deputy spotted Warren struggling with three other men outside a bar. Upon approaching Warren, he used a taser at least twice. Soon after additional officers arrived and arrested him, he lost consciousness and died at the hospital soon after. He was 43 years old. **Outcome:** An Alabama Bureau of Investigation probe; the sheriff's deputy was placed on paid leave.

Reynaldo Cuevas - New York, NY (Sep 7, 2012)

Cuevas was shot and killed by police as he was fleeing armed men attempting to rob the bodega he worked at. He was 20 years old. **Aftermath:** The Bronx District Attorney did not find the officer at fault and declined to move the case forward to a grand jury. His mother filed a $25 million wrongful death claim against the city last year or so.

Chavis Carter - Jonesboro, AK (July 29, 2012)

Police say Carter killed himself while handcuffed in the back of a police car. His mother pointed out that he was left-handed (he would have shot himself with his right hand), detained for marijuana while his concealed weapon supposedly went undetected, and not suicidal. Chavis was 21 years old. Aftermath: The officers involved were placed on administrative leave and the FBI stepped in to "monitor and assess" the situation. His mother filed a wrongful death suit.

Sharmel Edwards - Las Vegas, NV (Apr 21, 2012)

Edwards was suspected of stealing a vehicle. A police chase ensued. Cops said that when they were finally able to get her to leave her car, she pointed a gun at them, and they opened fire. At least three witnesses disputed that claim; with two saying she wasn't carrying a weapon at all. She was 49 years old. **Aftermath:** The Clark County DA office ruled that the officers who killed Edwards acted "reasonably and lawfully."

Tamon Robinson - New York, NY (Apr 18, 2012)

Police responded to a call from Canarsie, Brooklyn that Robinson was stealing paving stones. When confronted by police, Robinson, unarmed, ran toward the building where his mother lived; officers chased him by car, hitting him. Tamon was 27 years old. **Aftermath:** Robinson's family reached a $2 million settlement in a wrongful death suit against the city this year.

Ervin Jefferson - Atlanta, GA (Mar 24, 2012)

Security guards shot Jefferson to death during a "bizarre chain of events" outside of an apartment complex. He was 18 years old. **Aftermath:** Security guards Curtis Scott and Gary Jackson were arrested and charged with impersonating police.

Kendrec McDade - Pasadena, CA (Mar 24, 2012)

McDade was chased and shot by two police officers after a 911 caller falsely reported he had been robbed at gunpoint by two black men. Both were unarmed. McDade was shot seven times. He was 19 years old.

Aftermath: The police department and Los Angeles County District Attorney's Office cleared the officers of wrongdoing. Investigations by the FBI and Office of Independent Review were pending 2012.

Wendell Allen - New Orleans, LA (Mar 7, 2012)

Allen, unarmed, dressed only in jeans and sneakers, was shot and killed by New Orleans police officer Joshua Colclough executing a search warrant of Allen's home for marijuana. Allen was 20 years old. **Aftermath:** Colclough pleaded guilty to manslaughter and was sentenced to four years in prison last year.

Nehemiah Dillard - Gainesville, FL (Mar 5, 2012)

Dillard was admitted to Meridian Behavioral Healthcare after "displaying strange behavior" in a stranger's yard. He allegedly struck a member of the hospital's staff, who called police. Officers shot him twice with tasers after he allegedly attacked them. After being handcuffed, the Tampa Bay Times reports, "a staffer at the facility injected him with drugs" and Dillard died soon after from cardiac arrest.

Dante Price - Dayton, OH (Mar 1, 2012)

Security guards ordered Price out of an apartment complex. They told him to leave his car, but instead he decided to drive away, so they fired 17 shots at him. Dante was 25 years old. Aftermath: Justin Wissinger and Christopher Tarbert pled guilty to involuntary manslaughter and abduction. They were sentenced 3 to 11 years in prison.

Raymond Allen - Galveston, TX (Feb 27, 2012)

Police responded to a complaint from a hotel that Allen was repeatedly jumping from the second story. Two officers used a taser gun on him. He stopped breathing and died in the hospital. He was 34 years old. **Aftermath**: His wife filed a lawsuit against Galveston, the county, and taser gun's manufacturer.

Sgt. Manuel Loggins - Orange County, CA (Feb 7, 2010)

On a religious fast and off medication for ADHD, Loggins allegedly crashed into a gate an Orange County high school with his car carrying his two daughters. After walking to and returning from the school's athletic field with a Bible, he was approached by a police officer, who shot Loggins three times through his car window. He was unarmed. He was 31 years old. Aftermath: Orange County paid $4.4 million to Loggins' family in a settlement last year.

Ramarley Graham - New York, NY (Feb 2, 2012)

Graham was shot and killed by police in the Bronx, who chased him into his home without a warrant. He was unarmed. Graham was just

18 years old. Aftermath: The officer, Richard Haste, was initially indicted in 2012, but the case was later overturned. A second grand jury decided not to indict Haste. Graham's mother said just recently that the Justice Department will proceed with its own investigation.

Kenneth Chamberlain - White Plains, NY (Nov 19, 2011)

Chamberlain's Life Aid alert necklace was triggered by mistake, causing the police to respond. He refused to answer his door, saying he did not need help. Officer Steven Hart called Chamberlain a "nigger." The police broke down his door. They allege that Chamberlain attempted to charge them with a butcher knife. They tasered him and shot him dead. Aftermath: No indictment for Officer Anthony Carelli, who shot Chamberlain twice. Chamberlain's family filed a $21 million wrongful death suit.

Alonzo Ashley - Denver, CO (July 18, 2011)

Police were called by Denver Zoo security who were alarmed over Ashley's behavior. Ashley was confronted and tasered. He started convulsing and then stopped breathing. Alonzo was 29 years old. Aftermath: Ashley's death was ruled a homicide by the coroner, but no officers were charged. Ashley's family sued Denver and the zoo.

Kenneth Harding - San Francisco, CA (July 16, 2011)

Harding fled a routine Muni fare inspection. The police said that a shootout ensued; witnesses said that Harding did not have a weapon. According to police Cmdr. Mike Biel, the caliber of the bullet that killed Harding did not match the caliber used by police. "We believe that the fatal wound on Mr. Harding's body was self-inflicted," Biel said. Kenneth was 19 years old. **Aftermath:** Harding's mother filed federal wrongful death and civil rights lawsuits against San Francisco.

Raheim Brown - Oakland, CA (Jan 22, 2011)

During a struggle with the police, Brown was shot five times, including twice in the head. Police reports alleged that Brown was attempting to stab an officer with a screwdriver. Raheim Brown was 20 years old. Aftermath: No indictment for Officer Barhin Bhatt. The Oakland Unified School District settled with Brown's parents for $995,000.

Reginald Doucet - Los Angeles, CA (Jan 14, 2011)

Police responded to a "disturbing the peace" call, where Doucet was arguing with a taxi driver. Doucet had stripped down. Doucet reportedly resisted arrest, and a chase ensued. During a violent confrontation, the unarmed Doucet was fatally shot. Reginald was 25 years old. Aftermath: The Los Angeles Police Commission ruled that officer Aaron Goff was justified in shooting Doucet. A judge dismissed the wrongful death lawsuit filed by Doucet's family.

Derrick Jones - Oakland, CA (Nov 8, 2010)

Jones' neighbor accused him of assault. Police arrived and Jones fled. According to Officers Perez-Angeles and Daza-Quiroz, when they caught up with Jones, they thought that he was reaching for a gun, so they fired at him. Six of their nine shots hit Jones, who was unarmed. Derrick was 37 years old. **Aftermath:** No indictment. Oakland settled with Jones' parents and daughter for $225,000. His widow lost a $10 million civil suit.

Danroy Henry - Thornwood, NY (Oct 17, 2010)

Officer Aaron Hess shot Henry through the windshield of Henry's car as Henry drove during a chaotic altercation. He was 20 years old. Aftermath: No indictment for Hess. Henry's family filed a wrongful death suit.

Steven Eugene Washington - Los Angeles, CA (Mar 20, 2010)

Police officers spotted Washington on a Los Angeles street. He reportedly approached them, appearing to be removing something from his waistband. He was shot and killed. No weapon was found on him. Later, Washington's family revealed that he was autistic. Steven was 27 years old. Aftermath: Police Chief Charlie Beck recommended that Officers Allan Corrales and George Diego be cleared of charges, but the civilian commission that oversees the LAPD disagreed. Washington's mother received $950,000 in a settlement with Los Angeles.

Aaron Campbell - Portland, OR (Jan 29, 2010)

Campbell was shot in front of his apartment after being reported to the police as suicidal and possessing a gun. Campbell was unarmed. Campbell was walked backward with his hands behind his head. Officer Frashour told Campbell to put his hands straight in the air. When Campbell did not comply, Frashour shot him. He was 25 years old. Aftermath: No indictment for Frashour. He was fired for not following protocol, but then reinstated. Portland agreed to pay Campbell's family $1.2 million to settle their civil suit against the city.

Kiwane Carrington - Champaign, IL (Oct 9, 2009)

Police investigating a suspected break-in at a house encountered the unarmed Carrington. A scuffle ensued and Officer Daniel Norbits' gun "went off," killing Carrington. He was 15 years old. Aftermath: No indictment for Norbits, but he did receive a total of $423,697 in disability and worker's compensation payments. Carrington's family received $470,000 from Champaign in a settlement of their wrongful death lawsuit.

Victor Steen - Pensacola, FL (Oct 3, 2009)

Steen rode his bike as a cop chased him. Steen refused to stop, and so the cop, Jerald Ard, tasered him. Steen fell from his bike and Ard ran him over, killing him. Ard also may have planted a gun on Steen after his death. Sheen was just 17 years old. Aftermath: Ard was suspended from the force without pay for two weeks. The city of Pensacola paid Steen's mother a $500,000 settlement.

Shem Walker - New York, NY (July 11, 2009)

Walker was shot when trying to eject an undercover officer from his stoop. Walker was unarmed. Shem was 49 years old. Walker was shot when trying to eject an undercover officer from his stoop. Walker was unarmed.

DeAunta Terrel Farrow - West Memphis, AK (July 22, 2007)

Farrow was out walking with his 14-year-old cousin when gunned down by a police officer, Erik Sammis. Sammis claims that only after he shot Farrow did he realize that the gun Farrow was carrying was a toy. Farrow was 12 years old. Aftermath: Sammis wasn't indicted. He resigned from the force via a letter that contained the sentence, "Then there are others who are not rational and breed hate and racism in this community." Sammis and Jimmy Evans, who was also on duty with him July 22, 2007, were found not liable in Farrow's family's $250 million civil suit.

Sean Bell - New York, NY (Nov 25, 2006)

On the night before Bell's wedding, Bell and his friends attempted to flee the scene of escalating tension with the police. The police fired about 50 shots into Bell's car, killing him in the process. Bell was 23 years old. Aftermath: All three officers were acquitted on all charges. They and their commanding officer were fired/forced to resign. New York City agreed to pay Bell's family $3.25 million to settle their wrongful death suit.

Henry Glover - New Orleans, LA (Sep 2, 2005)

Glover was shot in the chest by NOPD officer David Warren at a strip mall in the days following Hurricane Katrina. Glover, with the help of a friend, attempted to get aid, and ended up handcuffed. He died. NOPD

Officer Greg McRae set fire to Glover's body in Glover's friend's car. Glover was 31 years old. Aftermath: David Warren was sentenced to 25 years and 9 months on a manslaughter conviction. Greg MacRae got 17 years and 3 months for obstruction of justice. About a year and a half later, the Fifth Circuit Court of Appeals vacated Warren's convictions and two of MacRae's, ordering new trials. Warren was acquitted in the retrial.

Ronald Madison & James Brisette-
New Orleans, LA (Sep 4, 2005)

Police received a call claiming gunfire on the Danziger Bridge. Police opened fire upon arriving in a Budget Rental Truck. They hit Brisette. Madison, who was developmentally disabled, fled. Two cops chased him down. One, Robert Faulcon, shot him. The other, Sgt. Kenneth Bowen, was convicted of stomping Madison on the back before he died. Madison was 40 and Brisette, just 17 years of age. Aftermath: That conviction was later overturned. Police attempted a cover up. Eventually five officers involved in the shooting were found guilty of various charges. Faulcon was sentenced to 65 years' imprisonment, Bowen and Sgt. Robert Gisevius received 40 years, Officer Anthony Villavaso got 38 years, and Arthur "Archie" Kaufman, who was the investigator placed on the case and eventually found guilty of conspiring to conceal evidence, received 6 years. A month later, the same judge that convicted them, Kurt Engelhardt, vacated their convictions and ordered a new trial as a result of the defendants' appeal and "highly unusual, extensive and truly bizarre actions" by prosecutors.

Travares McGill - Sanford, FL (July 18, 2005)

McGill was killed by 2 security guards when they open fired on the car he was driving at an apartment complex at 3:10am on a Saturday morning. The two guards told police they started shooting because they thought the driver was trying to run them over. But evidence showed that the bullet that hit and killed the teenager hit him in the middle of the back and that the guard kept firing even after the car was no longer headed toward them. McGill was 16 years old. This was the same city that later would become famous for the Trayvon Martin murder. **Aftermath:** The guards- Ansley and Swofford were finally charged in November of that year – Swofford with manslaughter and both Swofford and Ansley with shooting into an occupied vehicle. The case went to trial, but it was eventually dismissed by a judge who determined that it was a case of self-defense.

Timothy Stansbury, Jr. - New York, NY (Jan 24, 2004)

Officer Richard S. Neri Jr., testified that he shot the unarmed Stansbury by accident when Stansbury pushed open the rooftop door of a building Neri was patrolling. Timothy was 19 years old. Aftermath: Neri was not indicted. He was suspended for 30 days without pay and stripped of his gun permanently. The NYPD settled the wrongful death lawsuit of Stansbury's family for $2 million.

Ousmane Zongo - New York, NY (May 22, 2003)

Zongo was shot four times (twice in the back) by Officer Bryan Conroy during a police raid in a storage facility where Zongo worked.

Zongo was unarmed and his business (art and musical instrument reparation) had nothing to do with what the police were investigating (CD and DVD piracy). He was 43 years old. **Aftermath:** Conroy was convicted of criminally negligent homicide. He received five years' probation and lost his job. Zongo's family received $3 million in a wrongful death suit.

Orlando Barlow - Las Vegas, NV (Feb 28, 2003)

Barlow was hired to babysit seven children. After a supposed argument, his employer (the children's mother) called the police, saying that Barlow was holding her children hostage with a sawed-off shotgun. Police responded to the call. Barlow was shot while surrendering. He was unarmed. Barlow was 28 years old. Aftermath: A coroner's inquest labeled the shooting "excusable." The FBI looked into the matter. "The shooting was unanimously ruled justifiable, but Hartman and two other officers were fired after they printed T-shirts with the initials 'BDRT' — 'Baby's Daddy Removal Team' reported the Las Vegas Review-Journal.

Timothy Thomas - Cincinnati, OH (Apr 7, 2001)

Nine officers pursued Thomas, who was wanted on 14 misdemeanors. Twelve of them were traffic violations. A chase ensued. Thomas ran into an alley and was shot by Patrolman Stephen Roach, who joined the group of nine officers during the pursuit. Roach said he believed Thomas was going for a gun, but an investigation later revealed that Thomas was attempting to pull up his pants. Thomas was 19 years old. **Aftermath:** Roach was acquitted on a charge of negligent homicide. An investigation later revealed that Roach lied on his incident report and broke protocol.

Prince Jones- Fairfax County, VA (Sept 1, 2000

An undercover narcotics agent followed the unarmed Jones, firing 16 shots at him while Jones was in his Jeep. Eight landed. Officials later confirmed that Officer Carlton Jones (no relation) mistook Prince Jones for someone else. Prince was 25 years old. Aftermath: The Fairfax commonwealth's attorney and the Justice Department declined to file charges against the officer, Carlton Jones. The case was not put before a grand jury. Five years after the killing, Prince Jones's parents and daughter were awarded $3.7 million in a wrongful death lawsuit.

Ronald Beasley & Earl Murray - Dellwood, MO (June 12, 2000)

Beasley and Murray, described as family and friends as small-time drug dealers, were shot and killed during an attempted drug bust in a restaurant parking lot. One cop called the killings "unintended, but not a mistake." Beasley and Murray were both 36 years old. Aftermath: The officers were cleared of wrongdoing after a yearlong investigation.

Patrick Dorismond - New York, NY (Mar 16, 2000)

An undercover cop approached Dorismond and his friend, Kevin Kaiser, when they were standing outside of a lounge. The cop asked where he could buy marijuana. A scuffle ensued and another undercover cop, Anthony Vasquez, stepped in to help his partner. Vasquez claimed Dorismond grabbed his gun and caused it to discharge into his own chest. Vasquez said the first cop was in their face, and that he attempted to pull Dorismond out of the confrontation to no avail. Dorismond was 26 years old. **Aftermath:** Vasquez was not indicted. New York paid the Dorismond family $2.25 million as a settlement in a wrongful death suit.

Burns for News

Malcolm Ferguson - New York, NY (Mar 1, 2000)

Drug officers "noticed some movement" in the hallway of a public housing building and investigated. Ferguson, who was unarmed, ran up the stairs. "At some point, on the second-floor landing, there was a struggle," Chief John Scanlon said. "The [Officer Louis Rivera's] firearm discharged." Ferguson was 23 years old. Aftermath: Rivera was cleared of wrongdoing. Ferguson's mom, Juanita Young, was awarded $10.5 million as a result of her wrongful death suit against the NYPD and the city.

Amandou Diallo - New York, NY (Feb 4, 1999)

Four plainclothes officers fired a total of 41 shots at Diallo outside of his apartment in the Bronx. Nineteen hit him. He was armed with a wallet, which an officer mistook for a gun when he pulled it out of his pocket. Officers initially approached him because he supposedly matched the description of a serial rapist. Diallo was 23 years old. **Aftermath:** The officers were acquitted of all charges. Diallo's mother and stepfather filed a $61 million ($20m plus $1m for each shot fired) wrongful death suit against the officers and New York City. They settled for $3 million.

Note: Obviously there have been more deaths since I made this document that we can add, but I might be splitting hairs and truthfully do not have the time to add to it myself. I just wanted to make a note of it.

Appendix - B

"SAMPLE SYLLABUS SUPPLEMENT AND WRITING TEMPLATE: *Cognitive Climbing from and for Brain Diversity*"

STEP ONE: INTRODUCTION AND INFO RESOURCES

Go over the syllabus, "Cognitive Climbing from and for Brain Diversity", the below graphic of the "three pound" brain from https://askabiologist.asu.edu/what-your-brain-doing), and the required readings of: (1) "NEURO DIVERSITY" by Joseph Stevenson, Jay Finkelman, Bryant Horowitz, Melissa Druckrey and Karen Wilson Stevenson; (2) Stephen Pinker's "How the Mind Works"; and (3) "Mind: A Journey to the Heart of the Brain" by Daniel J. Siegel. Also explain the Instructor's role in using the PBS Series "The Brain" by David Eagleman (video) and National Geographic's "Mind: A Scientific Guide to Who You Are, How You Got That Way, and How to Make the Most of It" by Patricia Daniels (audio). Remind students that they will be asked to complete 10 (ten) reflective/reaction papers (two-three pages) to the readings from the assigned chapters (or other selected articles) pursuant to the "critical thinking and writing" template/guidelines in the syllabus.

Figure M: Lobes of the Human Brain

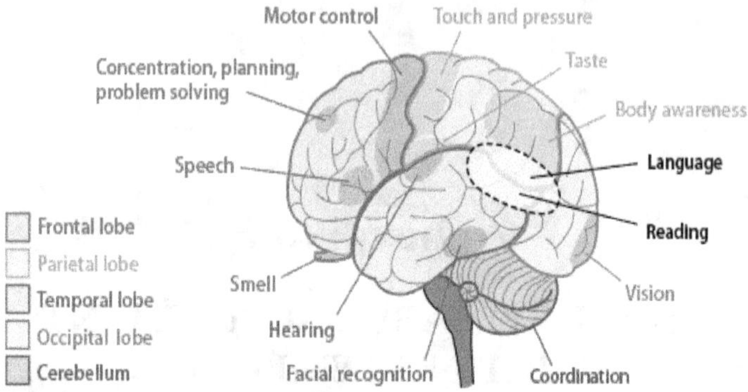

STEP TWO: GROUPING AND THE BRAIN

Survey the class to see what areas students are majoring in to determine transdisciplinary diversity. Introduce student groups to the use, application, relevance, and utility of theoretical frameworks or perspectives". Have a discussion with the students about how the world has become blended with transdisciplinary in nature. Cite examples from the National Geographic Guide. The common denominator of this transdisciplinarianism, however, is the human brain. Everyone has a brain; every discipline needs the brain; and every human challenge requires the brain. Have students sound off numbers from "1" to "5" with the first student as "1", second student as "2", third student as "3", etc. Assign and align each student with a group number, regional lobe of the brain, and hierarchal level of the taxonomy. The grouping should look something like the following:

Group One ("CRE"), Frontal Lobe, Creating Level

Group Two ("EVA"), Parietal Lobe, Evaluating Level

Group Three ("ANA"), Temporal Lobe, Analyzing Level

Group Four ("APP"), Occipital Lobe, Applying Level

Group Five ("UND"), Cerebellum, Understanding Level

STEP THREE: LIFE AND THE LIMBIC LOBE

Have each group go online from their cell phones and briefly research the cerebral capacity of the "Limbic Lobe". Hold a class wide discussion about the relationship of the Limbic Lobe to human emotions like happiness, love and sadness. Have them also go online to review the captured video of two separate incidents in April of 2017. The first is the incident where a 69-year-old Asian American physician was violently removed from an aircraft; the second is the incident with a 24-year-old African American man in Sacramento who was violently apprehended for jaywalking. Hold a discussion about the relevance and relationship of the Limbic Lobe in both instances. Have students discuss their own "lived experiences" with similar authorities. Have them discuss how both situations could have handled differently if all parties involved mindfully "thought things through thoroughly throughout" by leveraging the human brain for elevating higher order thinking, cognitive climbing, levitating upward from a guided taxonomy.

STEP FOUR: CLIMBING AND LEVITATING

Explain the history and purpose of the journal, BEFOREWARDS, then have students refer to and read the relevant pages of NEURO NOVO. Explain the relevance of the April, 20177 incidents and relationships between cognitive climbing and levitating taxonomies. Ask them to think about these areas in their own lives every time they take an elevator or staircase. Cognitive climbing from taxonomical levitation will help them reach clarity.

STEP FIVE: ASSIGNING AND ALIGNING GROUPS

Have each group remain the same for the term. Each group should use the term to become well-versed experts in their assigned taxonomical area. To this end, each group must develop of "knowledge repository" of their literature reviews. Students are strongly encouraged to use Pinker and Siegel books as resources and references. This will be relevant later in the term when all groups will critique the poster presentation proposals before finalization. Each group will be charged with identifying an incident to analyze against cognitive climbing and taxonomical levitation within the context of their regional lobe. Student groups can choose from the following incidents, chose one from our **Appendix A**, or identify a similar one on their own that better fits the context of their assigned regional lobe (like the recent incidents in Georgia or the incident with United Airlines, for instance):

Roseburg, Oregon
Sacramento, California
Ferguson, Missouri
New Your, New York
Dallas, Texas
Charleston, West Virginia
Charleston, North Carolina
Los Angeles, California
Chicago, Illinois
Baton Rouge, Louisiana
Minneapolis, Minnesota
San Bernardino, California
Sacramento, California
Fresno, California

The fundamental question is "how could this incident have "possibly" been prevented or handled differently if all persons "thought things through thoroughly throughout'? In the case of group one, from the perspective of speech, motor control and problem solving. In the case of group two, from the perspective of touch and body awareness. For group three, hearing and facial recognition. For group four, vision and sight. For group five, coordination and balance. Again, each group should use time over the course of the term to become experts in each group area assigned and the collected literature should, too, be put in each group's knowledge repository. Each "expert" group for the level of assigned taxonomy will critique that respective part of the group presentation (creating, evaluating, analyzing, applying, understanding) as well as provide feedback, insight, and input from their assigned regional lobe (frontal, parietal, temporal, occipital, cerebellum). All student group poster presentations will be presented at the last class to a wider audience of the academic community. As students develop their own framed upward taxonomies for bold new "thought leadership", there may be some cases or situations where a level of the taxonomy should be transitioned from the taxonomy to create a new one as the result of emerged complexity and required in depth analysis before levitating to the next level. We end here where we began by suggesting that living on God's beloved Earth is extremely hard work and living on His planet requires the unlocking and the emancipation of His blessed gift – the human brain – the core source for advancing human coherence, connectivity, cohesion and civility. The stakes are simply too high for all stakeholders across our beloved country to not respond to the ongoing and escalating crisis of human division and the so desperate need for engagement relative to human diversity. Indeed, this a serious challenge to our modern, anticipatory, and future civilization.

BRAIN REFLECTIVE / REACTION PAPERS (TWO-THREE PAGES)

(FROM: http://www.criticalthinking.org/pages/index-of-articles/1021/)

The Logic of "(Title of Text Chapter and/or Assigned Article)"

1. The main purpose of this chapter/article is ______________________________

(State as accurately as possible, the author's purpose for writing the chapter/article).

2. The key question that the author is addressing is ______________________________

(Figure out the key question in the mind of the author when he/she wrote the chapter/article)

3. The most important information in this chapter/ article is ______________________________

(Figure out the facts, experience, and data the author uses to support her/his conclusion)

4. The main inference/conclusions in this chapter/article are______________________________

(Identify the key conclusion the author comes to and presents in the chapter/article).

5.The key concepts(s) we need to understand in the chapter/article is (are)______________________________

By these concepts, the author means____

(Figure out the most important ideas you would have to understand to understand the author's line of reasoning).

6. The main assumption(s) underlying the author's thinking is (are)____

____

7a. If we take this line of reasoning seriously, the implications are

____

____

(What consequences are likely to follow if people take the author's line of reasoning seriously?)

7b. If we fail to take this line of reasoning seriously, the implications are

____

____

8. The main point(s) of view presented in this chapter/article is (are)

____

____

(What is the author looking at, and how is she/he seeing it?)

9. How does the text chapter/article relate to your assigned regional lobe, targeted level of taxonomy, and researched theoretical framework?

____

____

10. What are the related implications, benefits, impact, relevance and returns on investment if we take the author's underlying premises?

____

____

www.ingramcontent.com/pod-product-compliance
Lightning Source LLC
LaVergne TN
LVHW010533300926
849162LV00016B/1871/J
9781680534870